React: Cross-Platform Application Development with React Native

Harness the power of React Native to build 4 real-world apps

Emilio Rodriguez Martinez

BIRMINGHAM - MUMBAI

React: Cross-Platform Application Development with React Native

First published: March 2018

Production reference: 1070318

Published by Packt Publishing Ltd.
Livery Place, 35 Livery Street
Birmingham B3 2PB, UK.

ISBN: 978-1-78913-608-1

www.packtpub.com

Credits

This book is a blend of text and quizzes, all packaged up keeping your journey in mind. It includes content from the following Packt product:

React Native Blueprints by *Emilio Rodriguez Martinez*

Meet Your Expert

We have the best work of the following esteemed author to ensure that your learning journey is smooth:

Emilio Rodriguez Martinez is a senior software engineer who has been working on highly demanding JavaScript projects since 2010. He transitioned from web development positions into mobile development, first with hybrid technologies such as Cordova and then with native JavaScript solutions such as Titanium. In 2015, he focused on the development and maintenance of several apps built in React Native, some of which were featured in Apple's App Store as the top apps of the week. Nowadays, Emilio is part of the Red Hat mobile team, which leverages Red Hat's open source mobile platform. He serves as an advocate for mobile developers using RHMAP. He is also an active contributor to React Native's codebase and Stack Overflow, where he provides advice on React and React Native questions.

Table of Contents

Preface

React Native helps web and mobile developers to build cross-platform apps that perform at the same level as any other natively developed app. The range of apps that can be built using this library is huge. From e-commerce to games, React Native is a good fit for any mobile project due to its flexibility and extendable nature. There's no doubt React Native is not only a good alternative to native development, but also a great way to introduce web developers to a mobile project.

What's in It for Me?

Maps are vital for your journey, especially when you're holidaying in another continent. When it comes to learning, a roadmap helps you in giving a definitive path for progressing towards the goal. So, here you're presented with a roadmap before you begin your journey.

This book is meticulously designed and developed in order to empower you with all the right and relevant information on React Native. We've created this Learning Path for you that consists of four lessons:

Lesson 1, Project 1 – Car Booking App, explains how some of the most popular car-sharing apps can be developed using React Native.

Lesson 2, Project 2 – Image Sharing App, teaches you the fundamentals of how a social network based on image sharing can be created with React Native.

Lesson 3, Project 3 – Messaging App, shows you how to build a full-featured messaging app including push notifications and cloud-based storage.

Lesson 4, Project 4 – Game, shows you the fundamentals of how a 2D game can be developed using React Native.

What Will I Get from This Book ?

- Structure React Native projects to ease maintenance and extensibility
- Optimize a project to speed up development
- Use external modules to speed up the development and maintenance of your projects
- Explore the different UI and code patterns to be used for iOS and Android
- Know the best practices when building apps in React Native

Prerequisites

This book is for developers who want to build amazing cross-platform apps with React Native. Some of the prerequisites that is required before you begin this book are:

- Basic knowledge of HTML, CSS, and JavaScript is needed
- Prior working knowledge of React is assumed

Project 1 – Car Booking App

1

Considering the success of the React framework, Facebook recently introduced a new mobile development framework called React Native. With React Native's game-changing approach to hybrid mobile development, you can build native mobile applications that are much more powerful, interactive, and faster by using JavaScript.

In this lesson, we will set the focus on feature development rather than in building a user interface by delegating the styling of our applications to UI libraries such as native-base as well as spend more time in building custom UI components and screens.

The app we will build is a car booking app in which the user can select the location in which he/she wants to be picked up and the type of car she wants to book for the ride. Since we want to focus on the user interface, our app will only have two screens and a little state management is needed. Instead, we will dive deeper into aspects such as animations, component's layout, using custom fonts, or displaying external images.

The app will be available for iOS and Android devices, and since all the user interface will be custom made, 100% of the code will be reused between both platforms. We will only use two external libraries:

- `React-native-geocoder`: This will translate coordinates into human-readable locations
- `React-native-maps`: This will easily display the maps and the markers showing the locations for the bookable cars

Due to its nature, most of the car booking apps put their complexity in the backend code to connect drivers with riders effectively. We will skip this complexity and mock all that functionality in the app itself to focus on building beautiful and usable interfaces.

Overview

When building mobile apps, we need to make sure we reduce the interface complexity to the minimum, as it's often punishing to present the user intrusive manuals or tooltips once the app is open. It is a good practice to make our app self-explanatory, so the user can understand the usage just by going through the app screens. That's why using standard components such as drawer menus or standard lists is always a good idea, but is not always possible (as it happens in our current app) due to the kind of data we want to present to the user.

In our case, we put all the functionality in the main screen plus in a modal box. Let's take a look at what the app will look like on iOS devices:

The background on our main screen is the maps component itself where we will show all the available cars as markers in the map. On the maps, we will display three components:

- The pickup location box displaying the selected pickup location
- The location pin, which can be dragged around the maps to select a new location
- The selector for the kind of car the user wants to book. We will display three options: ECONOMY, SPECIAL, and SUPERIOR

Since most of the components are custom built, this screen will look very similar in any Android device:

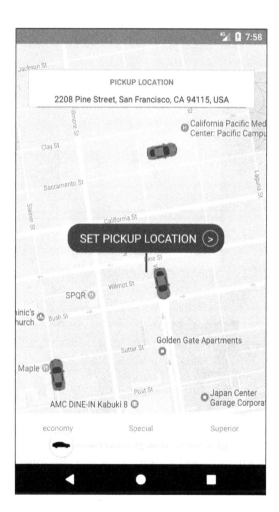

Setting up the Folder Structure

Let's initialize a React Native project using React Native's CLI. The project will be named `carBooking` and will be available for iOS and Android devices:

```
react-native init --version="0.49.3" carBooking
```

In this app, there is only one screen so that the folder structure for the code should be very straightforward. Since we will be using external images and fonts, we will organize these resources in two separate folders: `img` and `fonts`, both under the root folder.

The images and fonts used to build this app can be downloaded freely from some image and font sock websites. The name of the font we will use is **Blair ITC**.

We also stored the following images inside the `img` folder:

- `car.png`: A simple drawing of a car to represent the bookable cars on the map.
- `class.png`: The silhouette of a car to show inside the class selection button
- `classBar.png`: The bar in which the class selection button will be slid to change the class.
- `loading.png`: Our custom spinner. It will be stored as a static image and animated through the code.

Finally, let's take a look at our `package.json` file:

```
{
    "name": "carBooking",
    "version": "0.0.1",
    "private": true,
    "scripts": {
        "start": "node node_modules/react-native/local-cli/cli.js start",
        "test": "jest"
    },
    "dependencies": {
        "react": "16.0.0-beta.5",
        "react-native": "0.49.3",
"react-native-geocoder": " 0.4.8",
        "react-native-maps": " 0.15.2"
    },
    "devDependencies": {
        "babel-jest": "20.0.3",
        "babel-preset-react-native": "1.9.2",
```

```
        "jest": "20.0.4",
        "react-test-renderer": "16.0.0-alpha.6"
    },
    "jest": {
        "preset": "react-native"
    },
  "rnpm": {
        "assets": ["./fonts"]
    }
}
```

We only use two npm modules:

* `react-native-geocoder`: This translates coordinates into human-readable locations

* `react-native-maps`: This easily displays the maps and the markers showing the locations for the bookable cars

In order to allow the app to use custom fonts, we need to make sure they are accessible from the native side. For that, we need to add a new key to `package.json` named `rnpm`. This key will store an array of `assets` in which we will define our `fonts` folder. During build time, React Native will copy the fonts to a location from where they will be available natively and therefore usable within our code. This is only required by fonts and some special resources, but not by images.

Files and Folders Created by React Native's CLI

Let's take the chance of having a simple folder structure in this app to show what other files and folders are created by React Native's CLI when initializing a project through `react-native init <projectName>`.

__tests__/

React Native's CLI includes Jest as a developer dependency and, to get testing started, it includes a folder named `__tests__`, in which all tests can be stored. By default, React Native's CLI adds one test file: `index.js`, representing the initial set of tests. Developers can add later tests for any components in the app. React Native also adds a `test` script in our `package.json`, so we can run `npm run test` from the very first moment.

When React Native detects the app is running in a simulator, it enables a developer toolset available through a hidden menu, which can be accessed through the shortcuts *command + D* on iOS or *command + M* on Android (on Windows *Ctrl* should be used instead of *command*). This is how the developer menu looks like in iOS:

And this is how it looks like in the Android simulator:

The Developer Menu

In the process of building an app in React Native, the developer will have debugging needs. React Native fulfills these needs with the ability to remotely debug our apps in Chrome developer's tools or external applications such as React Native Debugger. Errors, logs, and even React components can be debugged easily as in a normal web environment.

On top of that, React Native provides a way to automatically reload our app each time a change is done saving the developers the task of manually reloading the app (which can be achieved by pressing *command + R* or *Ctrl + R*). There are two options when we set our app for automatic reloading:

- Live reload detects any changes we make in the app's code and resets the app to its initial state after reloading.

- Hot reload also detects changes and reloads the app, but keeps the current state of the app. This is really useful when we are implementing user flows to save the developer to repeat each step in the flow (for example, logging in or registering test users)

- Finally, we can start the performance monitor to detect possible performance issues when performing complex operations such as animations or mathematical calculations.

Creating our App's Entry Point

Let's start our app's code by creating the entry point for our app: `index.js`. We import `src/main.js` in this file to use a common root component for our code base. Moreover, we will register the app with the name `carBooking`:

```
/*** index.js ***/

import { AppRegistry } from 'react-native';
import App from './src/main';
AppRegistry.registerComponent('carBooking', () => App);
```

Let's start building our `src/main.js` by adding a map component:

```
/*** src/main.js ** */

import React from 'react';
import { View, StyleSheet } from 'react-native';
import MapView from 'react-native-maps';

export default class Main extends React.Component {
  constructor(props) {
    super(props);
    this.initialRegion = {
      latitude: 37.78825,
      longitude: -122.4324,
      latitudeDelta: 0.00922,
      longitudeDelta: 0.00421,
    };
  }

  render() {
    return (
      <View style={{ flex: 1 }}>
        <MapView
          style={styles.fullScreenMap}
          initialRegion={this.initialRegion}
        />
      </View>
    );
```

```
    }
}

const styles = StyleSheet.create({
fullScreenMap: {
    position: 'absolute',
    top: 0,
    bottom: 0,
    left: 0,
    right: 0,
  },
});
```

Instead of using libraries for styling, we will create our own styles using `StyleSheet`, a React Native API, which serves as an abstraction similar to CSS style sheets. With `StyleSheet`, we can create a style sheet from an object (through the `create` method), which can be used in our components by referring to each style by its ID.

This way, we can reuse the style code and make the code more readable as we will be using meaningful names to refer to each style (for example, `<Text style={styles.title}>Title 1</Text>`).

At this point, we will only create a style referred by the key `fullScreenMap` and make it as an absolute position by covering the fullscreen size by adding `top`, `bottom`, `left`, and `right` coordinates to zero. On top of this, we need to add some styling to our container view to ensure it fills the whole screen: `{flex: 1}`. Setting `flex` to `1`, we want our view to fill all the space its parent occupies. Since this is the main view, `{flex: 1}` will take over the whole screen.

For our map component, we will use `react-native-maps`, an open module created by Airbnb using native maps capabilities for Google and Apple maps. `react-native-maps` is a very flexible module, really well maintained, and fully featured so that it has become the de facto maps module for React Native. As we will see later in this lesson, `react-native-maps` requires the developer to run `react-native link` in order for it to work.

Apart from the style, the `<MapView/>` component will take `initialRegion` as a property to centre the map in a specific set of coordinates, which should be the current location of the user. For consistency reasons, we will locate the center of the map in San Francisco where we will also place some bookable cars:

```
/** * src/main.js ** */

import React from 'react';
```

```
import { View, Animated, Image, StyleSheet } from 'react-native';
import MapView from 'react-native-maps';

export default class Main extends React.Component {
  constructor(props) {
    super(props);
    this.state = {
carLocations: [
        {
          rotation: 78,
          latitude: 37.78725,
          longitude: -122.4318,
        },
        {
          rotation: -10,
          latitude: 37.79015,
          longitude: -122.4318,
        },
        {
          rotation: 262,
          latitude: 37.78525,
          longitude: -122.4348,
        },
      ],
    };
    this.initialRegion = {
      latitude: 37.78825,
      longitude: -122.4324,
      latitudeDelta: 0.00922,
      longitudeDelta: 0.00421,
    };
  }

  render() {
    return (
      <View style={{ flex: 1 }}>
        <MapView
          style={styles.fullScreenMap}
          initialRegion={this.initialRegion}
        >
          {this.state.carLocations.map((carLocation, i) => (
            <MapView.Marker key={i} coordinate={carLocation}>
              <Animated.Image
                style={{{
```

```
                    transform: [{ rotate: `${carLocation.rotation}deg`
}],
                  }}
                  source={require('../img/car.png')}
                />
              </MapView.Marker>
            ))}
          </MapView>
        </View>
      );
    }
  }

  ...
```

We have added an array of carLocations to be shown on the map as markers. Inside our render function, we will iterate over this array and place the corresponding <MapView.Marker/> in the provided coordinates. Inside each marker, we will add the image of the car rotating it by a specific number of degrees, so they match the streets directions. Rotating images must be done with the Animated API, which will be better explained later in this lesson.

Let's add a new property in our state to store a human-readable position for the location in which the map is centered:

```
/** * src/main.js ** */

import GeoCoder from 'react-native-geocoder';

export default class Main extends React.Component {
  constructor(props) {
    super(props);
    this.state = {
      position: null,

      ...

    };

    ...

  }

_onRegionChange(region) {
    this.setState({ position: null });
```

```
        const self = this;
        if (this.timeoutId) clearTimeout(this.timeoutId);
        this.timeoutId = setTimeout(async () => {
          try {
            const res = await GeoCoder.geocodePosition({
              lat: region.latitude,
              lng: region.longitude,
            });
            self.setState({ position: res[0] });
          } catch (err) {
            console.log(err);
          }
        }, 2000);
    }
componentDidMount() {
      this._onRegionChange.call(this, this.initialRegion);
    }

    render() {
      <View style={{ flex: 1 }}>
        <MapView
          style={styles.fullScreenMap}
          initialRegion={this.initialRegion}
onRegionChange={this._onRegionChange.bind(this)}
        >

        ...

        </MapView>
      </View>;
    }
}

...
```

To fill this state variable, we also created a function _onRegionChange, which uses the react-native-geocoder module. This module uses Google Maps reverse geocoding services to translate some coordinates into a human-readable location. Because it's a Google Service, we might need to add an API key in order to authenticate our app with the service. All the instructions to get this module fully installed can be found at its repository URL https://github.com/airbnb/react-native maps/blob/master/docs/installation.md.

We want this state variable to be available from the first mount of the main component, so we will call _onRegionChange in componentDidMount so that the name of the initial location is also stored in the state. Moreover, we will add the onRegionChange property on our <MapView/> to ensure the name of the location is recalculated every time the map is moved to show a different region, so we always have the name of the location in the center of the map in our position state variable.

As a final step on this screen, we will add all the subviews and another function to confirm the booking request:

```
/** * src/main.js ** */

...

import LocationPin from './components/LocationPin';
import LocationSearch from './components/LocationSearch';
import ClassSelection from './components/ClassSelection';
import ConfirmationModal from './components/ConfirmationModal';

export default class Main extends React.Component {
  ...

_onBookingRequest() {
    this.setState({
      confirmationModalVisible: true,
    });
  }

  render() {
    return (
      <View style={{ flex: 1 }}>
        ...

<LocationSearch
          value={
            this.state.position &&
            (this.state.position.feature ||
              this.state.position.formattedAddress)
          }
        />
        <LocationPin onPress={this._onBookingRequest.bind(this)} />
        <ClassSelection />
        <ConfirmationModal
          visible={this.state.confirmationModalVisible}
```

```
          onClose={() => {
            this.setState({ confirmationModalVisible: false });
          }}
        />
      </View>
    );
  }
}

...
```

We added four subviews:

- `LocationSearch`: The component in which we will show the user the location that is centered on the map so she can know the name of the location she is exactly requesting the pickup.

- `LocationPin`: A pinpointing to the center of the map, so the user can see on the map where she will request the pickup. It will also display a button to confirm the pickup.

- `ClassSelection`: A bar where the user can select the type of car for the pickup (economy, special, or superior).

- `ConfirmationModal`: The modal displaying the confirmation of the request.

The `_onBookingRequest` method will be responsible for bringing the confirmation modal up when a booking is requested.

Adding Images to Our App

React Native deals with images in a similar way as websites do: images should be placed in a folder inside the projects folder structure, and then they can be referenced from the `<Image />` (or `<Animated.Image />`) by the `source` property. Let's see an example from our app:

- `car.png`: This is placed inside the `img/` folder in the root of our project

- Then the image will be displayed by creating an `<Image/>` component using the `source` property:

```
<Image source={require('../img/car.png')} />
```

Notice how the `source` property doesn't accept a string, but a `require('../img/car.png')`. This is a special case in React Native and may change in future versions.

LocationSearch

This should be a simple textbox displaying the human-readable name of the location in which the map is centered. Let's take a look at the code:

```
/*** src/components/LocationSearch.js ** */

import React from 'react';
import {
  View,
  Text,
  TextInput,
  ActivityIndicator,
  StyleSheet,
} from 'react-native';

export default class LocationSearch extends React.Component {
  render() {
    return (
      <View style={styles.container}>
        <Text style={styles.title}>PICKUP LOCATION</Text>
        {this.props.value && (
          <TextInput style={styles.location} value={this.props.value}
/>
        )}
        {!this.props.value && <ActivityIndicator style={styles.
spinner} />}
      </View>
    );
  }
}

const styles = StyleSheet.create({
  container: {
    backgroundColor: 'white',
    margin: 20,
    marginTop: 40,
    height: 60,
    padding: 10,
    borderColor: '#ccc',
    borderWidth: 1,
  },
  title: {
    alignSelf: 'center',
    fontSize: 12,
```

```
      color: 'green',
      fontWeight: 'bold',
    },
    location: {
      height: 40,
      textAlign: 'center',
      fontSize: 13,
    },
    spinner: {
      margin: 10,
    },
  });
```

It receives only one property: `value` (the name of the location to be displayed). If it's not set, it will display a spinner to show activity.

Because there are many different styles to be applied in this component, it's beneficial to use the `StyleSheet` API to organize the styles in a key/value object and refer it from our `render` method. This separation between logic and style helps in readability of the code and also enables code reuse as the styles can be cascaded down to child components.

Aligning Elements

React Native uses Flexbox for setting up the layout of the elements in an app. This is mostly straightforward, but sometimes it can be confusing when it comes to aligning elements as there are four properties that can be used for this purpose:

- `justifyContent`: It defines the alignment of the child elements through the main axis
- `alignItems`: It defines the alignment of the child elements through the cross-axis
- `alignContent`: It aligns a flex container's lines within when there is extra space in the cross-axis
- `alignSelf`: It allows the default alignment (or the one specified by `alignItems`) to be overridden for individual flex items

The first three properties should be assigned to the container element, while the fourth one will be applied to a child element in case we want to override the default alignment.

In our case, we only want one element (the title) to be center aligned so we can use `alignSelf: 'center'`. Later in this lesson, we will see other uses for the different `align` properties.

LocationPin

In this section, we will focus on building the pinpointing to the center of the map to visually confirm the pickup location. This pin also contains a button, which can be used to trigger a pickup request:

```
/** * src/components/LocationPin.js ** */

import React from 'react';
import {
  View,
  Text,
Dimensions,
  TouchableOpacity,
  StyleSheet,
} from 'react-native';

const { height, width } = Dimensions.get('window');

export default class LocationPin extends React.Component {
  render() {
    return (
      <View style={styles.container}>
        <View style={styles.banner}>
          <Text style={styles.bannerText}>SET PICKUP LOCATION</Text>
<TouchableOpacity
          style={styles.bannerButton}
          onPress={this.props.onPress}
        >
          <Text style={styles.bannerButtonText}>{'>'}</Text>
        </TouchableOpacity>
        </View>
        <View style={styles.bannerPole} />
      </View>
    );
  }
}

const styles = StyleSheet.create({
  container: {
    position: 'absolute',
top: height / 2 - 60,
    left: width / 2 - 120,
  },
```

```
    banner: {
  flexDirection: 'row',
      alignSelf: 'center',
      justifyContent: 'center',
      borderRadius: 20,
      backgroundColor: '#333',
      padding: 10,
      paddingBottom: 10,
  shadowColor: '#000000',
      shadowOffset: {
        width: 0,
        height: 3,
      },
      shadowRadius: 5,
      shadowOpacity: 1.0,
    },
    bannerText: {
      alignSelf: 'center',
      color: 'white',
      marginRight: 10,
      marginLeft: 10,
      fontSize: 18,
    },
    bannerButton: {
      borderWidth: 1,
      borderColor: '#ccc',
      width: 26,
      height: 26,
      borderRadius: 13,
    },
    bannerButtonText: {
      color: 'white',
      textAlign: 'center',
  backgroundColor: 'transparent',
      fontSize: 18,
    },
    bannerPole: {
      backgroundColor: '#333',
      width: 3,
      height: 30,
      alignSelf: 'center',
    },
  });
```

This component is again very light in terms of functionality, but has a lot of custom style. Let's dive into some of the style details.

flexDirection

By default, React Native and Flexbox stack elements vertically:

For the banner in our pin, we want to stack every element horizontally after each other as follows:

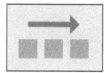

This can be achieved by adding the following styles to the containing element `flexDirection: 'row'`. The other valid options for `flexDirection` are:

* `row-reverse`
* `column` (default)
* `column-reverse`

Dimensions

One of the first lines of code in this component extracts the height and the width from the device into two variables:

```
const {height, width} = Dimensions.get('window');
```

Obtaining the height and width of the device enables us developers to absolute position some elements being confident they will show properly aligned. For example, we want the banner of our pin to be aligned in the center of the screen, so it points to the center of the map. We can do this by adding {top: (height/2), left: (width/2)} to the banner style in our style sheet. Of book, that would align the upper-left corner, so we need to subtract half the size of the banner to each property to ensure it gets centered in the middle of the element. This trick can be used whenever we need to align an element that is not relative to any other in the components tree although it is recommended to use relative positioning when possible.

Shadows

Let's set focus on our banner's style, specifically on the shadows properties:

```
banner: {
  ...
  shadowColor: '#000000',
  shadowOffset: {
    width: 0,
    height: 3
  },
  shadowRadius: 5,
  shadowOpacity: 1.0
}
```

In order to add a shadow to a component, we need to add four properties:

- shadowColor: This adds the hexadecimal or RGBA value of the color we want for our component
- shadowOffset: This shows how far we want our shadow to be casted
- shadowRadius: This shows the value of the radius in the corner of our shadow
- shadowOpacity: This shows how dark we want our shadow to be

That's it for our LocationPin component.

ClassSelection

In this component, we will explore the Animated API in React Native to get started with animations. Moreover, we will use custom fonts to improve the user experience and increase the feeling of customization in our app:

```
/*** src/components/ClassSelection.js ** */

import React from 'react';
import {
  View,
  Image,
  Dimensions,
  Text,
  TouchableOpacity,
Animated,
  StyleSheet,
} from 'react-native';

const { height, width } = Dimensions.get('window');

export default class ClassSelection extends React.Component {
  constructor(props) {
    super(props);
    this.state = {
classButtonPosition: new Animated.Value(15 + width * 0.1),
    };
  }

  _onClassChange(className) {
    if (className === 'superior') {
Animated.timing(this.state.classButtonPosition, {
        toValue: width * 0.77,
        duration: 500,
      }).start();
    }

    if (className === 'special') {
Animated.timing(this.state.classButtonPosition, {
        toValue: width * 0.5 - 20,
        duration: 500,
      }).start();
    }

    if (className === 'economy') {
Animated.timing(this.state.classButtonPosition, {
        toValue: 15 + width * 0.1,
        duration: 500,
      }).start();
    }
```

```
    }

  render() {
    return (
      <View style={styles.container}>
        <Image
          style={styles.classBar}
          source={require('../../img/classBar.png')}
        />
<Animated.View
          style={[styles.classButton, { left: this.state.
classButtonPosition }]}
        >
          <Image
            style={styles.classButtonImage}
            source={require('../../img/class.png')}
          />
        </Animated.View>
        <TouchableOpacity
          style={[
            styles.classButtonContainer,
            {
              width: width / 3 - 10,
              left: width * 0.11,
            },
          ]}
          onPress={this._onClassChange.bind(this, 'economy')}
        >
          <Text style={styles.classLabel}>economy</Text>
        </TouchableOpacity>
        <TouchableOpacity
          style={[
            styles.classButtonContainer,
            { width: width / 3, left: width / 3 },
          ]}
          onPress={this._onClassChange.bind(this, 'special')}
        >
          <Text style={[styles.classLabel, { textAlign: 'center' }]}>
            Special
          </Text>
        </TouchableOpacity>
        <TouchableOpacity
          style={[
            styles.classButtonContainer,
```

```
            { width: width / 3, right: width * 0.11 },
          ]}
          onPress={this._onClassChange.bind(this, 'superior')}
        >
          <Text style={[styles.classLabel, { textAlign: 'right' }]}>
            Superior
          </Text>
        </TouchableOpacity>
      </View>
    );
  }
}

const styles = StyleSheet.create({
  container: {
    height: 80,
    backgroundColor: 'white',
    position: 'absolute',
    bottom: 0,
    left: 0,
    right: 0,
    paddingBottom: 10,
  },
  classBar: {
width: width * 0.7,
    left: width * 0.15,
    resizeMode: 'contain',
    height: 30,
    top: 35,
  },
  classButton: {
    top: 30,
    justifyContent: 'center',
    borderRadius: 20,
    borderColor: '#ccc',
    borderWidth: 1,
    position: 'absolute',
    backgroundColor: 'white',
    height: 40,
    width: 40,
  },
  classButtonImage: {
    alignSelf: 'center',
    resizeMode: 'contain',
```

```
      width: 30,
    },
    classButtonContainer: {
      backgroundColor: 'transparent',
      position: 'absolute',
      height: 70,
      top: 10,
    },
    classLabel: {
      paddingTop: 5,
      fontSize: 12,
    },
});
```

This simple component is made out of five sub components:

- `classBar`: This is an image showing the bar and the stop points for each class
- `classButton`: This is the round button, which will be moved to the selected class once the user presses a specific class
- `classButtonContainer`: This is the touchable component detecting what class the user wants to select
- `classLabel`: These are titles for each class to be displayed on top of the bar

Let's start by taking a look at the styles as we can find a new property for image components: `resizeMode`, which determines how to resize the image when the frame doesn't match the raw image dimensions. From the five possible values (`cover`, `contain`, `stretch`, `repeat`, and `center`), we chose contain as we want to scale the image uniformly (maintain the image's aspect ratio) so that both dimensions of the image will be equal to or less than the corresponding dimension of the view. We are using these properties both in `classBar` and `classButtonImage` being the two images we will need to resize in this view.

Adding Custom Fonts

React Native includes a long list of cross-platform fonts available by default. The list of fonts can be checked on `https://github.com/react-native-training/react-native-fonts`.

Nevertheless, adding custom fonts is a common need when developing apps, especially when designers are involved, so we will use our car booking app as a playground to test this functionality.

Adding custom fonts to our app is a three steps task:

1. Add the font file (.ttf) into a folder inside our project. We used fonts/ for this app.

2. Add the following lines to our package.json:

```
"rnpm": {
    "assets": ["./fonts"]
}
```

3. Run the following command in a terminal:

```
react-native link
```

That's it, React Native's CLI will handle the insertion of the fonts folder and its files inside the iOS and Android project at once. Our fonts will be available by their font name (which may not be the same as the filename). In our case, we have fontFamily: 'Blair ITC' in our style sheet.

We can now modify our classLabel style in the ClassSelection component to include the new font:

```
    . . .

classLabel: {
    fontFamily: 'Blair ITC',
    paddingTop: 5,
    fontSize: 12,
},

    . . .
```

Animations

React Native's Animated API is designed to make it very easy to concisely express a wide variety of interesting animation and interaction patterns in a very performant way. Animated focuses on declarative relationships between inputs and outputs, with configurable transforms in between, and simple start/stop methods to control time-based animation execution.

What we want to do in our app is to move the classButton to a specific location whenever the user presses the class she wants to book. Let's take a closer look at how we are using this API in our app:

```
/** * src/components/ClassSelection ***/
```

```
...

export default class ClassSelection extends React.Component {
  constructor(props) {
    super(props);
    this.state = {
      classButtonPosition: new Animated.Value(15 + width * 0.1),
    };
  }

  _onClassChange(className) {
    if (className === 'superior') {
      Animated.timing(this.state.classButtonPosition, {
        toValue: width * 0.77,
        duration: 500,
      }).start();
    }

    ...

  }

  render() {
    return (
      ...

      <Animated.View style={{ left: this.state.classButtonPosition }}>
        <Image
          style={styles.classButtonImage}
          source={require('../../img/class.png')}
        />
      </Animated.View>

      ...

      <TouchableOpacity
        onPress={this._onClassChange.bind(this, 'superior')}
      >
        <Text>Superior</Text>
      </TouchableOpacity>

      ...

    );
  }
```

```
}

...
```

For this movement to happen correctly, we need to wrap the `classButtonImage` in `Animated.View` and provide an initial `Animated.Value` to it as a left coordinate. We will use `this.state.classButtonPosition` for this matter so that we can change it when the user selects a specific class.

We are ready to start our animation. It will be triggered by the `_onClassChange` method, as it is the one invoked when the user presses `classButtonContainer` (`<TouchableOpacity/>`). This method is calling the `Animated.timing` function passing two parameters:

- The animated value to drive (`this.state.classButtonPosition`)
- An object containing the end value and the duration of the animation

Invoking `Animated.timing` will result in an object containing the `start()` method, which we call right away to start the animation. React Native will then know that the `left` coordinate of the `Animated.View` needs to be slowly changed according to the provided parameters.

As this may feel a bit overcomplicated for a simple move animation, it allows a wide range of customization as chaining animations or modifying the easing functions. We will see a rotation animation later in this lesson.

ConfirmationModal

Our last component is a modal view, which will be opened once the user has pressed on the SET PICKUP LOCATION button on the location pin. We will display the modal and a custom activity indicator, which will use a complex animation setup to continuously rotate in its position:

```
/** * src/components/ConfirmationModal.js ***/

import React from 'react';
import {
Modal,
  View,
  Text,
  Animated,
  Easing,
  TouchableOpacity,
  StyleSheet,
```

```
} from 'react-native';

export default class ConfirmationModal extends React.Component {
  componentWillMount() {
    this._animatedValue = new Animated.Value(0);
  }

cycleAnimation() {
    Animated.sequence([
      Animated.timing(this._animatedValue, {
        toValue: 100,
        duration: 1000,
        easing: Easing.linear,
      }),
      Animated.timing(this._animatedValue, {
        toValue: 0,
        duration: 0,
      }),
    ]).start(() => {
      this.cycleAnimation();
    });
  }

componentDidMount() {
    this.cycleAnimation();
  }

  render() {
const interpolatedRotateAnimation = this._animatedValue.interpolate({
      inputRange: [0, 100],
      outputRange: ['0deg', '360deg'],
    });

    return (
<Modal
        animationType={'fade'}
        visible={this.props.visible}
        transparent={true}
      >
        <View style={styles.overlay}>
          <View style={styles.container}>
            <Text style={styles.title}>Contacting nearest car...</
Text>
<Animated.Image
```

```
                    style={[
                      styles.spinner,
                      { transform: [{ rotate: interpolatedRotateAnimation }]
        },
                    ]}
                    source={require('../../img/loading.png')}
                  />
                  <TouchableOpacity
                    style={styles.closeButton}
                    onPress={this.props.onClose}
                  >
                    <Text style={styles.closeButtonText}>X</Text>
                  </TouchableOpacity>
                </View>
              </View>
            </Modal>
          );
        }
      }

      const styles = StyleSheet.create({
        overlay: {
          flex: 1,
          backgroundColor: '#0006',
          justifyContent: 'center',
        },
        container: {
          backgroundColor: 'white',
          alignSelf: 'center',
          padding: 20,
          borderColor: '#ccc',
          borderWidth: 1,
        },
        title: {
          textAlign: 'right',
          fontFamily: 'Blair ITC',
          paddingTop: 5,
          fontSize: 12,
        },
        spinner: {
          resizeMode: 'contain',
          height: 50,
          width: 50,
          margin: 50,
```

```
      alignSelf: 'center',
    },
    closeButton: {
      backgroundColor: '#333',
      width: 40,
      height: 40,
      borderRadius: 20,
      justifyContent: 'center',
      alignSelf: 'center',
    },
    closeButtonText: {
      color: 'white',
      alignSelf: 'center',
      fontSize: 20,
    },
});
```

For this component, we are using the `<Modal />` component available in React Native to take advantage of its fade animation and visibility capabilities. The property `this.props.visible` will drive the visibility of this component as it is the parent who is aware of the pickup request from the user.

Let's focus again on animations as we want to do a more complex setup for the spinner showing activity. We want to display an endless rotating animation, so we need to systematically call our `start()` animation method. In order to achieve this, we created a `cycleAnimation()` method, which is called on the component mount (to get the animation started) and from the `Animated.timing` returned object as it is passed as a callback to be invoked every time the animation ends.

We are also using `Animated.sequence` to concatenate two animations:

- Moving from 0 degrees to 360 (in one second using a linear easing)
- Moving from 360 degrees to 0 (in 0 seconds)

This is required to repeat the first animation over at the end of each cycle.

Finally, we defined a variable named `interpolatedRotateAnimation` to store the interpolation from 0 degrees to 360, so it can be passed to the `transform/rotate` style defining what are going to be the available rotation values when animating our `Animated.Image`.

As an experiment, we can try and change loading.png with an alternative image and see how it gets animated. This can be easily achieved by replacing the `source` property in our `<Animated.Image />` component:

```
    . . .

            <Animated.Image
              style={[
                styles.spinner,
                { transform: [{ rotate: interpolatedRotateAnimation }]
    },
              ]}
    source={require('../../img/spinner.png')}
              />


    . . .
```

Summary

Using UI libraries such as `native-base` or `react-native-elements` saves a lot of time and maintenance hassle when we need to build apps, but the results end up having a standard flavor, which is not always desirable in terms of user experience. That's why learning how to manipulate the style of our apps is always a good idea, especially on teams where the design is provided by UX specialists or app designers.

In this lesson, we took a deep look into the folders and files created by React Native's CLI when initializing a project. Moreover, we familiarized ourselves with the developer menu and its debugging functionalities. When building our app we set the focus on the layouts and component styling, but also on how to add and manipulate animations to make our interface more appealing to the user. We took a look at Flexbox layout system and how to stack and center elements in our components. API's such as dimensions were used to retrieve the device width and height to perform positioning tricks on some components. You learned how to add fonts and images into our app and how to show them to improve the user experience.

Now that we know how to build more custom interfaces, let's build in the next lesson an image sharing app in which design plays a key role.

Assessments

1. Why does the `react-native-geocoder` module uses Google Maps reverse geocoding services?

    1. To store a human-readable position for the location in which the map is centred
    2. To translate some coordinates into a human-readable location
    3. To add an API key in order to authenticate our app with the service
    4. To ensure the name of the location is recalculated every time the map is moved to show a different region

2. Which of the following properties is used for aligning elements?

    1. `justifyContent`
    2. `alignLeft`
    3. `alignRight`
    4. `alignJustify`

3. By default, React Native and Flexbox stack elements _____.

    1. Diagonally
    2. Reverse
    3. Vertically
    4. Horizontally

4. Which of the following lines of code extracts the height and the width from a device into two variables?

    1. `const {height, width} = Dimensions.get('height, width');`
    2. `constant {height, width} = Dimensions.get('window');`
    3. `const {height, width} = get('window');`
    4. `const {height, width} = Dimensions.get('window');`

5. Which are the four properties in order to add a shadow to a component?

2
Project 2 – Image Sharing App

At this point, we know how to create a fully-featured app with a custom interface. You even learned how to add a state management library to control shared data in our app so that the code base remains maintainable and scalable.

In this lesson, we will focus on building the app with a different state management library (Redux), using the camera capabilities, writing platform-specific code, and diving deeper into building a custom user interface, which is both appealing and usable. An image sharing app will serve as a good example for these features and also will set up the basis for understanding how big apps should be built on React Native.

We will reuse most of our code for the two platforms where this app will be available: iOS and Android. Although most of our user interface will be custom, we will use native-base to simplify UI elements as icons. For navigation, we will use react-navigation again as it provides the most commonly used navigation for each platform: tabbed navigation for iOS and drawer menu navigation for Android. Finally, we will use react-native-camera to handle the interaction with the device's camera. This will not only reduce implementation complexity but also will provide us with a large set of features for free that we could use to extend our app in the future.

For this app, we will mock up a number of API calls so that we don't need to build a backend. These calls should be easily replaced by real API when the time to build a connected app comes.

Overview

One of the main requirements when building an image sharing app is an appealing design. We will follow the design patterns for some of the most popular image sharing apps, adapting those patterns for each platform while trying to reuse as much code as possible taking advantage of React Native's cross-platform capabilities.

Let's first take a look at the user interface in iOS:

The main screen shows a simple header and a list of images, including the user picture, name, and a **More** icon to share the image. At the bottom, the tabbed navigation displays three icons representing the three main screens: **All Images**, **My Images**, and **Camera**.

[All images used for this sample app are free to be used in any form.]

When a user presses the **More** icon for a specific image, the **Share** menu will be displayed:

This is a standard iOS component. It doesn't make much sense to use it on a simulator, it can be better tested on an actual device.

Let's take a look at the second screen, **My Images**:

This is a grid representation of all the images uploaded by the current user, which can be updated by the next screen, **Camera**:

The iOS simulator doesn't include support for any camera, so this feature is again better tested on an actual device, although `react-native-camera` is fully usable and will return fake data when accessed. We will use a static image for testing purposes.

That's all for iOS; let's move now to the Android version:

As Android encourages drawer-based navigation instead of tabs, we will include a drawer menu icon in the header and will also make the camera available through a different icon.

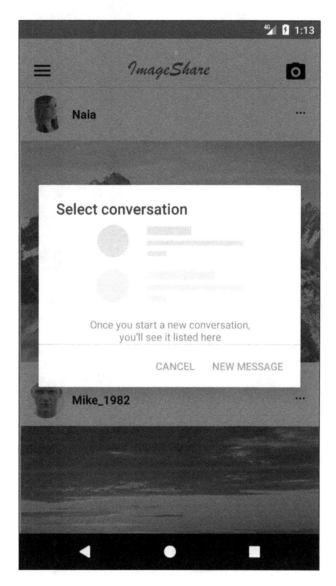

As with the iOS **Share** menu, Android has its own controller, so we will take advantage of this feature and include it whenever a user taps on the **More** icon on a specific image:

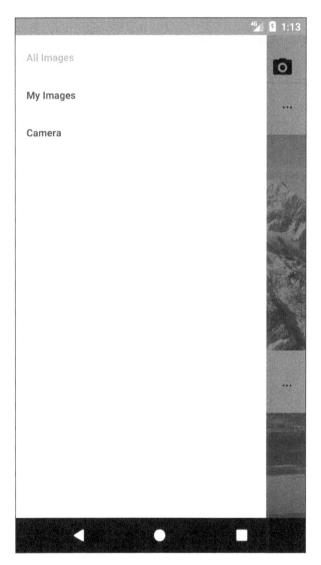

When a user taps on the drawer menu icon, the menu will be displayed, revealing the three available screens. From here, the user can navigate to the **My Images** screen:

Finally, the camera screen will also be accessible through the drawer menu:

The Android Simulator includes a camera simulation consisting of a colored moving square, which can be used for testing. Instead, we will stick with the fixed image we used in the iOS version for consistency reasons.

We will be covering the following topics in this lesson:

- Redux in React Native
- Using the camera

- Platform-specific code
- Drawer and tabbed navigation
- Sharing data with other apps

Setting up the Folder Structure

Let's initialize a React Native project using React Native's CLI. The project will be named `imageShare` and will be available for iOS and Android devices:

```
react-native init --version="0.44.0" imageShare
```

In order to use some packages in this app, we will be using a specific version of React Native (`0.44.0`).

We will be using Redux for our app, so we will create a folder structure in which we can accommodate our `reducers`, `actions`, `components`, `screens`, and `api` calls:

Moreover, we have added `logo.png` in the `img` folder. For the rest, we have a very standard React Native project. The entry point will be `index.ios.js` for iOS and `index.android.js` for Android:

```
/*** index.ios.js and index.android.js ***/

import { AppRegistry } from 'react-native';
import App from './src/main';

AppRegistry.registerComponent('imageShare', () => App);
```

We have the same implementation for both files as we want to use `src/main.js` as the common entry point for both platforms.

Let's jump into our `package.json` file to understand which dependencies we will have in our app:

```
/*** package.json ***/

{
        "name": "imageShare",
        "version": "0.0.1",
        "private": true,
        "scripts": {
                "start": "node node_modules/react-native/
                local-cli/cli.js start",
                "test": "jest"
        },
```

```
"dependencies": {
        "native-base": "^2.1.5",
        "react": "16.0.0-alpha.6",
        "react-native": "0.44.0",
        "react-native-camera": "^0.8.0",
        "react-navigation": "^1.0.0-beta.9",
        "react-redux": "^5.0.5",
        "redux": "^3.6.0",
        "redux-thunk": "^2.2.0"
},
"devDependencies": {
        "babel-jest": "20.0.3",
        "babel-preset-react-native": "1.9.2",
        "jest": "20.0.3",
        "react-test-renderer": "16.0.0-alpha.6"
},
"jest": {
        "preset": "react-native"
}
}
```

Some of the dependencies, such as `react-navigation` or `native-base`, are old acquaintances from previous lessons. Others, such as `react-native-camera`, will be introduced in this lesson for the first time. Some of them are closely related to the state management library we will be using for this app, Redux:

- `redux`: This is the state management library itself

- `react-redux`: These are the React handlers for Redux

- `redux-thunk`: This is Redux middleware that handles asynchronous action execution

To complete the installation, we will need to link `react-native-camera` as it requires some changes in the native part of our app:

```
react-native link react-native-camera
```

On iOS 10 and higher, we also need to modify our `ios/imageShare/Info.plist` to add a **Camera Usage Description**, which should be displayed to request permission to enable the camera within the app. We need to add these lines right before the last `</dict></plist>`:

```
<key>NSCameraUsageDescription</key>
<string>imageShare requires access to the camera on this device to perform this action</string>
```

```
<key>NSPhotoLibraryUsageDescription</key>
<string>imageShare requires access to the image library on this device
to perform this action</string>
```

Redux

Redux is a predictable state container for JavaScript apps based on simple principles:

- The whole state of your app is stored in an object tree inside a single **store**
- The only way to change the state tree is to emit an **action**, an object describing what happened
- To specify how the actions transform the state tree, you write pure **reducers**

Its popularity comes from the degree of consistency, testability, and developer experience that can be derived from its use in any kind of code base (frontend or backend). It's also simple to reason and master due to its strict unidirectional data flow:

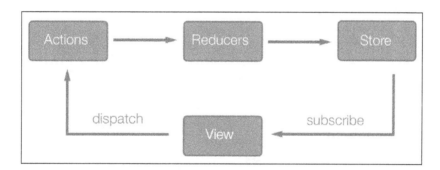

User triggers and **Actions** that are processed by **Reducers**, which are just pure functions applying changes to the state based on that **Action**. The resulting state is saved in a single **Store**, which is used by the **View** in our app to display the current state of the application.

Redux is a complex topic that falls out of the scope of this book, but it will be extensively used throughout some of the lessons in this book, so it could be beneficial to take a look at their official documentation (`http://redux.js.org/`) to get acquainted with the basic concepts of this state management library.

Some of the basic concepts of Redux will be used in our `src/main.js` file:

```
/*** src/main.js ***/

import React from 'react';
```

```
import { DrawerNavigator,TabNavigator } from 'react-navigation';
import { Platform } from 'react-native';

import { Provider } from 'react-redux';
import { createStore, combineReducers, applyMiddleware } from 'redux';
import thunk from 'redux-thunk';
import imagesReducer from './reducers/images';

import ImagesList from './screens/ImagesList.js';
import MyImages from './screens/MyImages.js';
import Camera from './screens/Camera.js';

let Navigator;
if(Platform.OS === 'ios'){
  Navigator = TabNavigator({
    ImagesList: { screen: ImagesList },
    MyImages: { screen: MyImages },
    Camera: { screen: Camera }
  }, {
    tabBarOptions: {
      inactiveTintColor: '#aaa',
      activeTintColor: '#000',
      showLabel: false
    }
  });
} else {
  Navigator = DrawerNavigator({
    ImagesList: { screen: ImagesList },
    MyImages: { screen: MyImages },
    Camera: { screen: Camera }
  });
}let store = createStore(combineReducers({ imagesReducer }),
applyMiddleware(thunk));

export default class App extends React.Component {
  render() {
    return (
      <Provider store={store}>
        <Navigator/>
      </Provider>
    )
  }
}
```

Let's focus first on the Redux ceremony. `let store = createStore(combineReducers({ imagesReducer }), applyMiddleware(thunk));` sets up the store by combining the imported reducers (we only have one reducer for this app, so this is merely informative) and applying the **Thunk** middleware, which will enable our app to use asynchronous actions. We will simulate several API calls that will return asynchronous promises, so this middleware is needed to properly handle the resolutions of those promises.

Then, we have our `render` method:

```
<Provider store={store}>
   <Navigator/>
</Provider>
```

This is standard in most Redux apps using React. We wrap the root component (`<Navigator />` in our case) with a `<Provider />` component to ensure that we will have the `store` available from the root of our app. The Redux `connect` method will be available for us to use in our containers or screens as we proceed in this lesson.

We will use a `<Navigator />` component as the root of our app, but it will have a different nature based on which platform is running:

```
let Navigator;
if(Platform.OS === 'ios'){
  Navigator = TabNavigator({


    ...


  });
} else {
  Navigator = DrawerNavigator({


    ...


  });
}
```

`Platform` is a React Native API used mainly to identify which platform our app is running on. We can write iOS-specific code by enclosing that code with `if(Platform.OS === 'ios'){ ... }` and the same goes for Android: `if(Platform.OS === 'android'){ ... }`.

In this case, we are using it to build a tabbed navigator on iOS and a drawer
navigator on Android, which are the **de facto** navigation patterns for those
platforms. On both navigators, we will set ImagesList, MyImages, and Camera as the
three main screens in our app.

ImagesList

The main screen in our app is a list of images retrieved from the backend. We will
display this images together with their corresponding uploader profile pictures and
names. For each image, we will show More, which can be used to share the image
with other apps on the user's device, such as messaging apps or social networks.
Most of the UI for this screen will be derived from the <Gallery /> component, so
we will focus on connecting the screen with Redux store, adding a custom header,
and a scroll view to make the gallery scrollable, and adding an activity indicator to
warn the user about network activity:

```
/*** src/components/ImagesList ***/

import React from 'react';
import { View, ScrollView } from 'react-native';

import { bindActionCreators } from 'redux';
import { connect } from 'react-redux';
import * as Actions from '../actions';
import { Icon } from 'native-base';

import Header from '../components/Header';
import Gallery from '../components/Gallery';
import ActivityIndicator from '../components/ActivityIndicator';

class ImagesList extends React.Component {
  static navigationOptions = {
    tabBarIcon: ({ tintColor }) => (
      <Icon name='list' style={{fontSize: 40, color: tintColor}}/>
    ),
    drawerLabel: 'All Images'
  };

  componentWillMount() {
    this.props.fetchImages();
  }

  componentWillReceiveProps(nextProps) {
```

```
      if(!this.props.addingImage && nextProps.addingImage) {
        this.scrollable.scrollTo({y: 0});
      }
    }

  render() {
    return (
      <View style={{flex: 1}}>
        <Header onMenuButtonPress={() =>
        this.props.navigation.navigate('DrawerOpen')}
        onCameraButtonPress={() =>
        this.props.navigation.navigate('Camera')}/>
<ScrollView ref={(scrollable) => {
          this.scrollable = scrollable;
        }}>
          { this.props.addingImage && <ActivityIndicator
            message='Adding image' /> }
          <Gallery imageList={this.props.images} loading=
          {this.props.fetchingImages}/>
        </ScrollView>
      </View>
    );
  }
}

function mapStateToProps(state) { return { images: state.
imagesReducer.images, addingImage: state.imagesReducer.addingImage,
fetchingImages: state.imagesReducer.fetchingImages } }
function mapStateActionsToProps(dispatch) { return
bindActionCreators(Actions, dispatch) }

export default connect(mapStateToProps, mapStateActionsToProps)
(ImagesList);
```

As most of the React apps use Redux, we need to connect our component with
the state and the actions. We will create two functions (mapStateToProps and
mapStateActionsToProps) to decorate our <ImageList /> component with the
mapped actions and parts of the state the component is interested in:

- images: This is the list of images we will use to render in our <Gallery />

- addingImage: This is a flag we will set to true when uploading an image

- fetchingImages: This is a flag that will be set to true when the app requests
  the list of images to the backend in order to update the store

The only action we will need on this screen is `fetchImages`, which is accessible through the `props``component` because we connected the list of actions in `Actions` to our `<ImagesList />` component. On a similar note, we have the three state variables (`images`, `addingImage`, and `fetchingImages`) available through `props`, thanks to the same `connect` invocation:

```
function mapStateToProps(state) {
  return {
    images: state.imagesReducer.images,
    addingImage: state.imagesReducer.addingImage,
    fetchingImages: state.imagesReducer.fetchingImages
  };
}
function mapStateActionsToProps(dispatch) {
  return bindActionCreators(Actions, dispatch);
}

export default connect(mapStateToProps, mapStateActionsToProps)
(ImagesList);
```

That's all we need from Redux. We will see this pattern in other screens as well, as it's a common solution for connecting React components with parts of the store and the list of actions.

The `fetchImages` action is called on `componentWillMount` as the initial retrieval of the list of images to be rendered:

```
componentWillMount() {
    this.props.fetchImages();
}
```

We also added a way to detect the moment the `addingImage` flag is set to `true` to display the activity indicator:

```
componentWillReceiveProps(nextProps) {
  if(!this.props.addingImage && nextProps.addingImage) {
    this.scrollable.scrollTo({y: 0});
  }
}
```

This method will call `scrollTo` in the `<Scrollview />` to make sure it displays the top part, so the `<ActivityIndicator />` is visible to the user. We are using a custom `<ActivityIndicator />` this time (imported from `src/components/ActivityIndicator`), as we want to display not only a spinner but also a message.

Last, we will add two components:

- `<Header />`: This displays the logo and (in the Android version) two icons to navigate to the drawer menu and the camera screen
- `<Gallery />`: This shows the formatted list of images and uploaders

Before moving to another screen, let's take a look at the three custom components we included in this one: `<ActivityIndicator />`, `<Header />`, and `<Gallery />`.

Gallery

Gallery holds all the rendering logic for the list of images. It relies on `native-base` and, more specifically, on two of its components, `<List />` and `<ListItem />`:

```
/*** src/components/Gallery ***/

import React from 'react';
import { List, ListItem, Text, Icon, Button, Container, Content }
 from 'native-base';
import { Image, Dimensions, View, Share, ActivityIndicator, StyleSheet
} from 'react-native';

var {height, width} = Dimensions.get('window');

export default class Gallery extends React.Component {
  _share(image) {
    Share.share({message: image.src, title: 'Image from: ' +
                image.user.name})
  }

  render() {
    return (
      <View>
        <List style={{margin: -15}}>
          {
            this.props.imageList && this.props.imageList.map((image)
=>
            {
              return (
                <ListItem
                    key={image.id}
                    style={{borderBottomWidth: 0,
                    flexDirection: 'column', marginBottom: -20}}>
                  <View style={styles.user}>
```

```
                        <Image source={{uri: image.user.pic}}
                          style={styles.userPic}/>
                        <Text style={{fontWeight: 'bold'}}>
                        {image.user.name}</Text>
                    </View>
                    <Image source={{uri: image.src}}
                    style={styles.image}/>
                    <Button style={{position: 'absolute', right: 15,
                    top: 25}} transparent
                    onPress={this._share.bind(this, image)}>
                        <Icon name='ios-more' style={{fontSize: 20,
                        color: 'black'}}/>
                    </Button>
                </ListItem>
            );
          })
        }
      </List>
      {
        this.props.loading &&
        <View style={styles.spinnerContainer}>
          <ActivityIndicator/>
        </View>
      }
    </View>
    );
  }
}

const styles = StyleSheet.create({
  user: {
    flexDirection: 'row',
    alignSelf: 'flex-start',
    padding: 10
  },
  userPic: {
    width: 50,
    height: 50,
    resizeMode: 'cover',
    marginRight: 10,
    borderRadius: 25
  },
  image: {
    width: width,
```

```
      height: 300,
      resizeMode: 'cover'
    },
    spinnerContainer: {
      justifyContent: 'center',
      height: (height - 50)
    }
  });
```

This component takes two props from its parent: `loading` and `imageList`.

`loading` is used to display a standard `<ActivityIndicator />` showing the user network activity. This time we are using the standard one instead of a custom indicator as it should be clear enough what the network activity is indicating.

`imageList` is the array storing the list of images, which will be rendered in our `<Gallery />` one `<ListenItem />` at a time. Each `<ListItem />` holds a `<Button />` with `onPress={this._share.bind(this, image)` to share the image with other apps. Let's take a look at the `_share` function:

```
_share(image) {
  Share.share({message: image.src, title: 'Image from: '
              + image.user.name})
}
```

`Share` is a React Native API for sharing text content. In our case, we will share the URL (`img.src`) of the image together with a simple title. Sharing text is the easiest way of sharing content between apps, as many apps would accept text as a shared format.

It's also worth noting the style we apply to the image to take over the whole width and a fixed height (`300`), so we have a stable layout for all images even when the display images have different sizes. For this setup, we use `resizeMode: 'cover'` so the images are not stretched in any dimension. This means we may end up cutting the image, but it compensates on uniformity. Another option would be to use `resizeMode: contain` if we don't want to cut anything, but rather want to fit the image inside these bounds while possibly shrinking them.

Header

We want to reuse a custom header between several screens. That's why it's best to create a separate component for it and import it in those screens:

```
/*** src/components/Header ***/
```

```
import React from 'react';
import { View, Image, StyleSheet } from 'react-native';
import { Icon, Button } from 'native-base';
import { Platform } from 'react-native';

export default class Header extends React.Component {
  render() {
    return (
      <View style={styles.container}>
        {
          Platform.OS === 'android' &&
          <Button transparent onPress={this.props.onMenuButtonPress}>
            <Icon android='md-menu' style={styles.menuIcon}/>
          </Button>
        }
        <Image source={require('../../img/logo.png')}
          style={styles.logo} />
        {
          Platform.OS === 'android' &&
          <Button onPress={this.props.onCameraButtonPress}
transparent>
            <Icon name='camera' style={styles.cameraIcon}/>
          </Button>
        }
      </View>
    );
  }
}

const styles = StyleSheet.create({
  container: {
    paddingTop: 20,
    flexDirection: 'row',
    alignItems: 'center',
    justifyContent: 'space-around',
    borderBottomWidth: 1,
    borderBottomColor: '#ccc'
  },
  menuIcon: {
    fontSize: 30,
    color: 'black'
  },
  logo: {
    height: 25,
```

```
      resizeMode: 'contain',
      margin: 10
    },
    cameraIcon: {
      fontSize: 30,
      color: 'black'
    }
  });
```

We are using the Platform API again to detect Android devices and show a drawer menu button and a camera button only on that platform. We decided to do this to make those features, which are the core of the app, more prominent to Android users by reducing the number of buttons needed to be pressed to reach them. The actions to be performed when pressing the buttons are passed by the parent component through two props:

* onMenuButtonPress

* onCameraButtonPress

Those two props call two separate functions invoking the navigate method of the navigator:

* this.props.navigation.navigate('DrawerOpen')

* this.props.navigation.navigate('Camera')

The last thing to note is how we set up the layout for the container in this component. We use justifyContent: 'space-around', which is the way we tell Flexbox to evenly distribute items in the line with equal space around them. Note that, visually, the spaces aren't equal since all the items have equal space on both sides. The first item will have one unit of space against the container edge, but two units of space between the next item because that next item has its own spacing that applies:

ActivityIndicator

Our custom ActivityIndicator is a very simple component:

```
/*** src/components/ActivityIndicator ***/
```

```
import React from 'react';
import { ActivityIndicator, View, Text, StyleSheet }
from 'react-native';

export default class CustomActivityIndicator extends React.Component {
  render() {
    return (
      <View style={styles.container}>
        <ActivityIndicator style={{marginRight: 10}}/>
        <Text>{this.props.message}</Text>
      </View>
    );
  }
}

const styles = StyleSheet.create({
  container: {
    flexDirection: 'row',
    justifyContent: 'center',
    padding: 10,
    backgroundColor: '#f0f0f0'
  }
});
```

It receives a message as a prop and displays it next to a standard spinner. We also added a custom background color (#f0f0f0) to make it more visible over the white backgrounds.

Let's move now to the camera screen to add our images to the list.

Camera

Most of the logic when taking photos can be abstracted when using react-native-camera, so we will focus on using this module in our component and making sure we connect it to our app's state through Redux actions:

```
/*** src/screens/Camera ***/

import React, { Component } from 'react';
import {
  Dimensions,
  StyleSheet,
  Text,
  TouchableHighlight,
```

```
    View
} from 'react-native';
import { Button, Icon } from 'native-base';
import Camera from 'react-native-camera';
import { bindActionCreators } from 'redux';
import { connect } from 'react-redux';
import * as Actions from '../actions';

class CameraScreen extends Component {
  static navigationOptions = {
    tabBarIcon: ({ tintColor }) => (
      <Icon name='camera' style={{fontSize: 40, color: tintColor}}/>
    ),
  };

  render() {
    return (
      <View style={styles.container}>
        <Camera
          ref={(cam) => {
            this.camera = cam;
          }}
          style={styles.preview}
          aspect={Camera.constants.Aspect.fill}>
          <Button onPress={this.takePicture.bind(this)}
          style={styles.cameraButton} transparent>
            <Icon name='camera' style={{fontSize: 70,
            color: 'white'}}/>
          </Button>
        </Camera>
        <Button onPress={() =>
         this.props.navigation.navigate('ImagesList')}
         style={styles.backButton} transparent>
          <Icon ios='ios-arrow-dropleft' android='md-arrow-dropleft'
           style={{fontSize: 30, color: 'white'}}/>
        </Button>
      </View>
    );
  }

  takePicture() {
    const options = {};
    this.camera.capture({metadata: options})
      .then((data) => {
```

```
            this.props.addImage(data);
            this.props.navigation.navigate('ImagesList');
        })
        .catch(err => console.error(err));
    }
}

const styles = StyleSheet.create({
  container: {
    flex: 1,
    flexDirection: 'row',
  },
  preview: {
    flex: 1,
    justifyContent: 'flex-end',
    padding: 20
  },
  capture: {
    flex: 0,
    backgroundColor: '#fff',
    borderRadius: 5,
    color: '#000',
    padding: 10,
    margin: 40
  },
  cameraButton: {
    flex: 0,
    alignSelf: 'center'
  },
  backButton: {
    position: 'absolute',
    top:20
  }
});

function mapStateToProps(state) { return {} }
function mapStateActionsToProps(dispatch) { return
bindActionCreators(Actions, dispatch) }

export default connect(mapStateToProps, mapStateActionsToProps)
(CameraScreen);
```

The way `react-native-camera` works is by providing a component we can include in our screen and, through a reference, we can call its `capture` method, which returns a promise we can use to call `addImage` to upload our image to the app's backend.

Let's take a closer look at the `<Camera />` component:

```
<Camera
    ref={(cam) => {
      this.camera = cam;
    }}
    style={styles.preview}
    aspect={Camera.constants.Aspect.fill}>


...


</Camera>
```

The `<Camera />` component takes three props:

* `ref`: This sets a reference to the `<Camera />` component in the parent component for it to call the capture method.

* `style`: This allows the developer to specify the look of the component in the app.

* `aspect`: This allows you to define how the view renderer will behave when displaying camera's view. There are three options: `fill`, `fit`, and `stretch`.

The `takePicture` function will be invoked when the user presses the camera button:

```
takePicture() {
    const options = {};
    this.camera.capture({metadata: options})
    .then((data) => {
      this.props.addImage(data);
      this.props.navigation.navigate('ImagesList');
    })
    .catch(err => console.error(err));
}
```

We will use the saved reference to the camera to call its `capture` method to which we can pass some metadata (for example, the location in which the photo was taken). This method returns a promise, which will be resolved with the image data so we will use this data to call the `addImage` action to send this data to the backend, so the picture can be added to the `imagesList`. Right after sending the image to the backend, we will make the app navigate back to the `ImagesList` screen. The `addImage` method will set the `addingImages` flag, so the `ImageList` screen can display the activity indicator with the corresponding message.

Let's move on to the last screen in our app: `MyImages`.

MyImages

This screen shows all the images the logged user has uploaded. We are using fake images for this screen to pre-fill this screen, but more images can be added through the camera screen.

Most of the rendering logic will be moved to a separate component named `<ImagesGrid />`:

```
/*** src/screens/MyImages ***/

import React from 'react';
import {
  Image,
  TouchableOpacity,
  Text,
  View,
  ActivityIndicator,
  Dimensions
} from 'react-native';

import { bindActionCreators } from 'redux';
import { connect } from 'react-redux';
import * as Actions from '../actions';
import { Icon } from 'native-base';

import Header from '../components/Header';
import ImagesGrid from '../components/ImagesGrid';

var {height, width} = Dimensions.get('window');

class MyImages extends React.Component {
  static navigationOptions = {
```

```
      drawerLabel: 'My Images',
      tabBarIcon: ({ tintColor }) => (
        <Icon name='person' style={{fontSize: 40, color: tintColor}}/>
      )
    };

    componentWillMount() {
      this.props.fetchImages(this.props.user.name);
    }

    render() {
      return (
        <View>
          <Header onMenuButtonPress={() =>
          this.props.navigation.navigate('DrawerOpen')}
          onCameraButtonPress={() =>
          this.props.navigation.navigate('Camera')}/>
          {
            this.props.fetchingImages &&
            <View style={{justifyContent: 'center',
             height: (height - 50)}}>
              <ActivityIndicator/>
            </View>
          }
          <ImagesGrid images={this.props.images}/>
        </View>
      );
    }
  }

  function mapStateToProps(state) { return { images: state.
  imagesReducer.userImages, user: state.imagesReducer.user,
  fetchingImages: state.imagesReducer.fetchingUserImages } }
  function mapStateActionsToProps(dispatch) { return
  bindActionCreators(Actions, dispatch) }

  export default connect(mapStateToProps, mapStateActionsToProps)
  (MyImages);
```

The first thing this component does is make a call to the `fetchImages` action but,
unlike the `<ImagesList />` component, it passes the username to only retrieve the
pictures for the logged in user. When we create this action, we need to take this into
account and receive an optional `userName` parameter to filter out the list of images
we will retrieve.

Other than that, this component delegates most of its behavior to `<ImageGrid />` so that we can reuse the render capabilities for other users. Let's move on to `<ImageGrid />`.

ImageGrid

A simple scroll view and a list of images. This component is as simple as that, but it's configured in a way that allows the images to flow like a grid in an easy way:

```
/*** src/components/ImageGrid ***/

import React from 'react';
import {
  Image,
  TouchableOpacity,
  ScrollView,
  Dimensions,
  View,
  StyleSheet
} from 'react-native';

var {height, width} = Dimensions.get('window');

export default class ImagesGrid extends React.Component {
  render() {
    return (
      <ScrollView>
        <View style={styles.imageContainer}>
          {
            this.props.images &&
            this.props.images.map(img => {
              return (<Image style={styles.image}
              key={img.id} source={{uri: img.src}}/>);
            })
          }
        </View>
      </ScrollView>
    );
  }
}

const styles = StyleSheet.create({
  imageContainer: {
```

```
          flexDirection: 'row',
          alignItems: 'flex-start',
          flexWrap: 'wrap'
        },
        image: {
          width: (width/3 - 2),
          margin: 1,
          height: (width/3 - 2),
          resizeMode: 'cover'
        }
    });
```

When styling the container, we use `flexWrap: 'wrap'` to ensure the images flow not only in the `row` direction but also spread to new lines when the device width is covered for a line of images. By setting `width` and `height` for each image to `width/3 - 2`, we ensure the container can fit three images per row, including two pixels for a small margin between them.

There are also several grid modules available through `npm`, but we have decided to build our own component for this matter, as we don't need extra functionality in the grid and we gain the flexibility to do it this way.

Those were all the screens and visual components we need in our image share app. Let's take a look now at the glue that makes them work together, the actions and the reducers.

Actions

As we see on our screens, there are only two actions needed for this app, `fetchImages` (for all users or for a specific user) and `addImage`:

```
/*** src/actions/index ***/

import api from '../api';

export function fetchImages(userId = null) {
  let actionName, actionNameSuccess, actionNameError;
  if(userId) {
    actionName = 'FETCH_USER_IMAGES';
    actionNameSuccess = 'FETCH_USER_IMAGES_SUCCESS';
    actionNameError = 'FETCH_USER_IMAGES_ERROR';
  } else {
    actionName = 'FETCH_IMAGES';
    actionNameSuccess = 'FETCH_IMAGES_SUCCESS';
```

```
        actionNameError = 'ADD_IMAGE_ERROR';
    }

    return dispatch => {
      dispatch({ type: actionName });
      api
        .fetchImages(userId)
        .then(images => {
          dispatch({
            type: actionNameSuccess,
            images
          })
        })
        .catch(error => {
          dispatch({
            type: actionNameError,
            error
          });
        });
    };
}

export function addImage(data = null) {
  return dispatch => {
    dispatch({ type: 'ADD_IMAGE' });
    api
      .addImage()
      .then(imageSrc => {
        dispatch({
          type: 'ADD_IMAGE_SUCCESS',
          imageSrc
        });
      })
      .catch(error => {
        dispatch({
          type: 'ADD_IMAGE_ERROR',
          error
        });
      });
  };
}
```

Redux actions are just simple objects describing an event, including its payload. Since we are using `redux-thunk`, our **action creators** will return a function in which the Redux `dispatch` function will be called, passing the action. Let's take a closer look at our `addImage` action:

```
export function addImage(data = null) {
  return dispatch => {
    dispatch({ type: 'ADD_IMAGE' });
    api
      .addImage()
      .then(imageSrc => {
        dispatch({
          type: 'ADD_IMAGE_SUCCESS',
          imageSrc
        });
      })
      .catch(error => {
        dispatch({
          type: 'ADD_IMAGE_ERROR',
          error
        });
      });
  };
}
```

The function we return starts by dispatching an action named `ADD_IMAGE` with no payload, as we just want to let Redux know that we are ready to make a network request to upload the image to our backend. Then, we make that request using our `api` (we will mock this call later). This request will return a promise, so we can attach `.then` and `.catch` callbacks to handle the response. If the response is positive (the image was properly uploaded), we will dispatch an `ADD_IMAGE_SUCCESS` action passing the URL for the uploaded image. If there is an error, we will dispatch an `ADD_IMAGE_ERROR` action covering all the possible states.

Most of the action creators work in a similar way when making network requests in **Redux** and **Thunk**. In fact, our action `fetchImages` is very similar to `addImage`, with one exception: it needs to check if `userId` was passed and issued a different set of actions instead, so the reducers can modify the state accordingly. Let's then take a look at the reducers, which will be handling all these actions.

Reducers

In Redux, reducers are functions in charge of updating the state as new actions happen. They receive the current state and the action (including any payload) and return a new state object. We won't go deep into how reducers work, we just need to understand their basic structure:

```
/*** src/reducers/index ***/

const initialState = {
  images: null,
  userImages: null,
  error: null,
  user: {
    id: 78261,
    name: 'Sharer1',
    pic: 'https://cdn.pixabay.com/photo/2015/07/20/12/53/
          man-852762_960_720.jpg'
  }
}

export default function (state = initialState, action) {
  switch(action.type){
    case 'FETCH_IMAGES':
      return Object.assign({}, state, {
        images: [],
        fetchingImages: true,
        error: null
      });
    case 'FETCH_IMAGES_SUCCESS':
      return Object.assign({}, state, {
        fetchingImages: false,
        images: action.images,
        error: null
      });
    case 'FETCH_IMAGES_ERROR':
      return Object.assign({}, state, {
        fetchingImages: false,
        images: null,
        error: action.error
      });
    case 'FETCH_USER_IMAGES':
      return Object.assign({}, state, {
        userImages: [],
```

```
        fetchingUserImages: true,
        error: null
      });
    case 'FETCH_USER_IMAGES_SUCCESS':
      return Object.assign({}, state, {
        fetchingUserImages: false,
        userImages: action.images,
        error: null
      });
    case 'FETCH_USER_IMAGES_ERROR':
      return Object.assign({}, state, {
        fetchingUserImages: false,
        userImages: null,
        error: action.error
      });
    case 'ADD_IMAGE':
      return Object.assign({}, state, {
        addingImage: true,
        error: null
      });
    case 'ADD_IMAGE_SUCCESS':
      let image = {
        id: Math.floor(Math.random() * 99999999),
        src: action.imageSrc,
        user: state.user
      }
      return Object.assign({}, state, {
        addingImage: false,
        images: [image].concat(state.images),
        userImages: [image].concat(state.images),
        error: null
      });
    case 'ADD_IMAGE_ERROR':
      return Object.assign({}, state, {
        addingImage: false,
        error: action.error
      });
    default:
      return state;
  }
}
```

Let's break this down:

```
const initialState = {
  images: null,
  userImages: null,
  error: null,
  user: {
    id: 78261,
    name: 'Sharer1',
    pic: 'https://cdn.pixabay.com/photo/2015/07/20/12/53/
        man-852762_960_720.jpg'
  }
}
```

We start with an initial state where all properties will be set to `null` except for `user`, which will contain mocked user data. This initial state is injected by default in the reducer on startup:

```
export default function (state = initialState, action) {

  ...

}
```

In the subsequent calls, Redux will inject the actual state after applying any actions. Inside this function, we have `switch` evaluating the type of each triggered action to modify the state according to that action and its payload. Let's take, for example, the `FETCH_IMAGES_SUCCESS` action:

```
case 'FETCH_IMAGES_SUCCESS':
  return Object.assign({}, state, {
    fetchingImages: false,
    images: action.images,
    error: null
  });
```

One of the rules in Redux is that reducers shouldn't mutate state, but return a new object after an action is triggered. Using `Object.assign`, we return a new object containing the current state plus the desired changes based on the action which just happened. In this case, we are setting the `fetchingImages` flag to `false` to let our components know that they can hide any activity indicator related to the action of fetching images. We also set the received list of images (from `actions.images`) in the key `images` of our state, so they can be injected into the components requiring them. Finally, we set the `error` flag to `null` to hide any errors we may have displayed because of a previous state.

As we mentioned before, every asynchronous action should be split into three separate actions to represent the three different states: asynchronous request pending, succeeded, and errored. This way, we will have three groups of actions for our app:

- `FETCH_IMAGES`, `FETCH_IMAGES_SUCCESS`, and `FETCH_IMAGES_ERROR`

- `FETCH_USER_IMAGES`, `FETCH_USER_IMAGES_SUCCESS`, and `FETCH_USER_IMAGES_ERROR`

- `ADD_IMAGE`, `ADD_IMAGE_SUCCESS`, and `ADD_IMAGE_ERROR`

It's important to note that we have separate cases for `FETCH_IMAGES` and `FETCH_USER_IMAGES`, as we want to keep two separate lists of images at the same time:

- A general one containing the images of all the people the user is following

- The list of the pictures the user has uploaded

The last missing piece is the API calls invoked from the action creators.

API

In a real-world app, we would place all the calls to our backend in a separate `api` folder. For educational purposes, we just mocked the two API calls that are core to our app, `addImage` and `fetchImages`:

```
/*** src/api/index ***/

export default {
  addImage: function(image) {
    return new Promise((resolve, reject) => {
      setTimeout(()=>{
        resolve( '<imgUrl>' );
      }, 3000)
    })
  },
  fetchImages: function(user = null){
    const images = [

      {id: 1, src: '<imgUrl>', user: {pic: '<imgUrl>', name: 'Naia'}},
      {id: 2, src: '<imgUrl>', user: {pic: '<imgUrl>',
       name: 'Mike_1982'}},
      {id: 5, src: '<imgUrl>', user: {pic: '<imgUrl>',
       name: 'Sharer1'}},
```

```
          {id: 3, src: '<imgUrl>', user: {pic: '<imgUrl>', name: 'Naia'}},
          {id: 6, src: '<imgUrl>', user: {pic: '<imgUrl>',
           name: 'Sharer1'}},
          {id: 4, src: '<imgUrl>', user: {pic: '<imgUrl>',
           name: 'Sharer1'}},
          {id: 7, src: '<imgUrl>', user: {pic: '<imgUrl>',
           name: 'Sharer1'}}

      ]
      return new Promise((resolve, reject) => {
        setTimeout(()=>{
          resolve( images.filter(img => !user || user === img.user.name)
          );
        }, 1500);
      })
    }
  }
```

To simulate the network delay, we added some `setTimeouts` that will help in testing the activity indicators we set up to show the user network activity. We also used promises instead of plain callbacks to make our code easier to read. We also skipped the image URLs in these examples to make it more succinct.

Summary

We used Redux in this app, and that shaped the folder structure we use. Although using Redux requires some boilerplate code, it helps break up our codebase in a reasonable way and removes direct dependencies between containers or screens. Redux is definitely a great addition when we need to maintain a shared state between screens, so we will be using it further throughout the rest of this book. In more complex apps, we would need to build more reducers and possibly separate them by domain and use Redux `combineReducers`. Moreover, we would need to add more actions and create separate files for each group of actions. For example, we would need actions for login, logout, and register, which we could put together in a folder named `src/actions/user.js`. Then, we should move our image-related actions (currently in `index.js`) to `src/actions/images.js`, so we can modify `src/actions/index.js` to use it as a combinator for the user and images actions in case we want to have the ability to import all the actions in one go.

Redux also helps with testing as it isolates the app's business logic into the reducers, so we can focus on testing them thoroughly.

Mocking the API calls enables us to build a quick prototype for our app. When a backend is available, we can reuse those mockups for test purposes and replace `src/api/index.js` with real HTTP calls. In any case, it's a good idea to have a separate folder for all our API calls, so we can replace them easily if there are any backend changes.

You also learned how to build platform-specific code (Android-specific in our case), which is a very useful feature for most apps. Some companies prefer to write separate apps for each platform and only reuse their business logic code, which should be very easy in any Redux-based app as it resides in the reducers.

There is no specific API in React Native to control the device's camera, but we can use the `react-native-camera` module for it. This is an example of a library accessing iOS- and Android-native APIs to expose them in the React Native JavaScript world.

In our next lesson, we will explore and cross that bridge between the native and the JavaScript world in React Native apps by building a messaging application.

Assessments

1. Actions that are processed by _____ are just pure functions that apply changes to the state based on that action.
    1. Viewer
    2. Reducers
    3. Navigator
    4. Middleware

2. Gallery holds all the rendering logic for the list of images. It relies on _____ and, more specifically, on two of its components, `<List />` and `<ListItem />`.
    1. native-base
    2. base-native
    3. resizeMode
    4. header

3. State whether the following statement is True or False: Every time a new message is stored in Firebase, `this.selectedChatMessages` will be synced to reflect it.

4. Which among the following is a `<TextInput/>` property that will be invoked when a user presses the **Return** or **Next** button on the keyboard?

   1. `this.refs.loginPassword.focus()`

   2. `React.Component`

   3. `onSubmitEditing`

   4. `onChangeText`

5. While splitting the login screen in two forms: `<LoginForm />` and `<RegistrationForm />` which three property components need to be passed?

Project 3 – Messaging App

One-to-one communication is the main use for mobile phones although, text messaging has been quickly replaced by direct messaging apps. In this lesson, we will build a messaging app in React Native with the support of Firebase, a mobile backend as a service that will free us from having to build a whole backend for our app. Instead, we will focus on handling the state of our app fully from the frontend. Of book, this may have security implications that need to be eventually tackled, but to keep the focus of this book on React Native's capabilities, we will stick with the approach of keeping all the logic inside our app.

Firebase is a real-time database built on self-synching collections of data, it plays very well with MobX, so we will use it again for controlling the state of our app. But in this lesson, we will dive deeper as we will build larger data stores, which will be injected in our component tree through the mobx-react connectors.

We will build the app to be used both with iOS and Android having some platform-specific code for navigation (we will use tabbed navigation for iOS and drawer navigation for Android).

To reduce the size of the code, in this lesson, we will set the focus on functionality rather than design. Most of the user interface will be plain and simple, but trying to keep usability in mind. Moreover, we will use a `react-native-gifted` chat for our chat screen--a pre-built React Native component to render chat rooms based on a list of messages.

Overview

A messaging app requires more work than the apps we reviewed in previous lessons, as it needs a user management system comprising of logging in, registering, and logging out. We will reduce the complexity of building this system using Firebase as a backend. Together with its user management system, we will use their push notifications system to notify users when new messages are sent to them. Firebase also gives an analytics platform, a lambda functions service, and a storage system for free, but the feature we will take the most profit from is their real-time database. We will store our user's profile, messages, and chats data there.

Let's take a look at what our app will look like to have a mental image of the screens we will be building:

First screen will be a login/registration screen because we need our users to provide a name and some credentials to attach their device to a specific account, so they can receive push notifications for each message they need to receive. Both authentication methods are validated using Firebase's API and would result in the chats screen when they are successful:

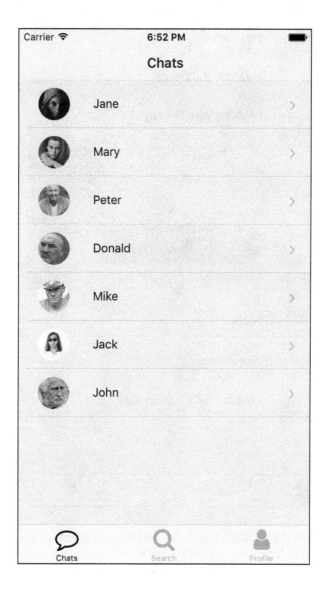

When pressing a contact in the contacts list, the app will display the conversation with the selected contact in the chat screen:

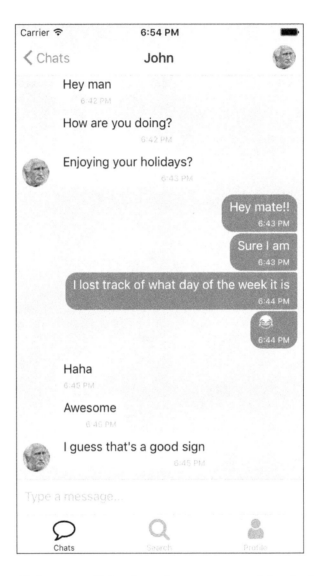

The chats screen will show up all the chats that were started for the logged in user. Initially, this screen will be empty as the user won't have initiated any chats. To start a conversation, the user should go to the search screen in order to find some contacts:

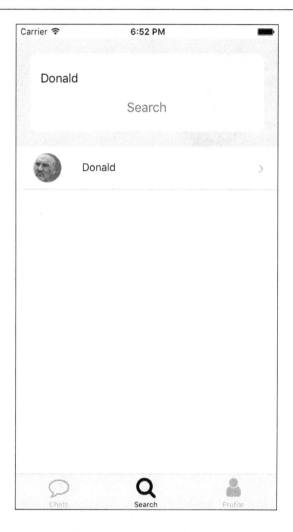

This is a simple screen where the user can enter the contact name to search for it in the database. If there is a match on the name of the contact; the user will be able to tap on it to get the conversation started. From that point on, the conversation will show in the chat screen.

The last screen is the profile screen:

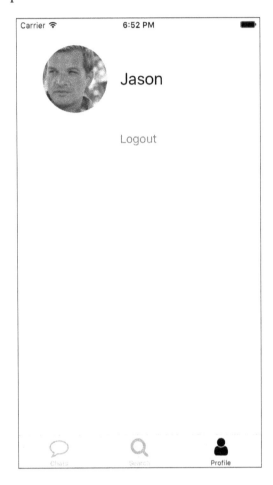

This screen is just a mean to log the current user out. When extending the app, we could add more features such as changing the avatar or the username.

While the app will look very similar on Android, navigation will be replaced by a drawer from which all the screens will be available. Let's take a look at the Android version:

The login/registration screen has standard text input and button components for Android:

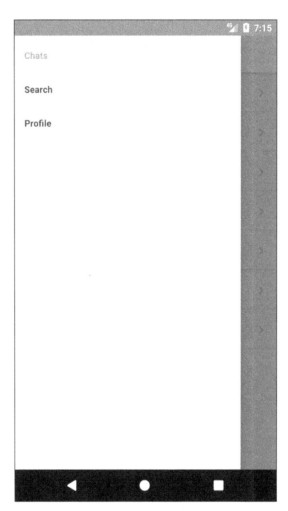

Once the user logs in, he/she can navigate through all the screens by opening the drawer through the sliding finger gesture. The screen that opens by default after login is the chats screens where we will list the list of open conversations the user has:

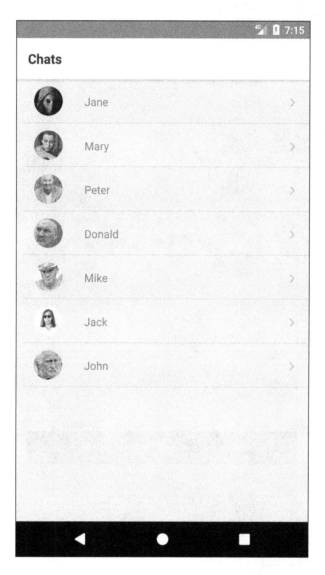

From this screen, the user can press a specific conversation to list the messages on it:

The next screen is the search screen, which will be used to search for other users and start conversations with them:

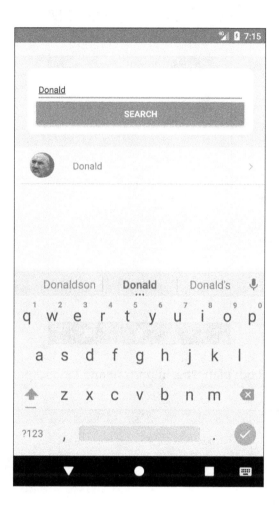

The last screen is the profile screen where the **LOGOUT** button can be found:

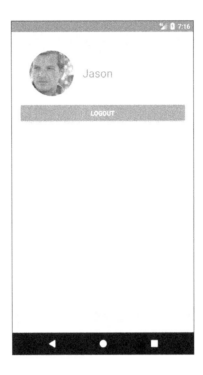

The app will work on both platforms in portrait and landscape mode out of the box:

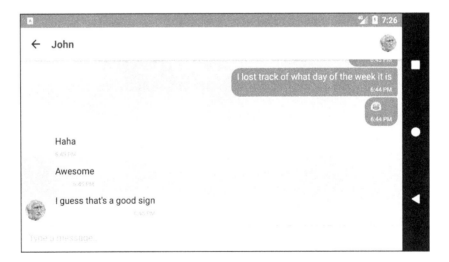

As we can imagine, this app will require of a powerful backend environment to store our users, messages, and statuses. Moreover, we will require a Push Notifications platform to notify users when they receive any messages. Since we are focusing in React Native in this book, we will delegate all this backend work to one of the most popular **Mobile Backend as a Services (MBaaS)** in the mobile world: Firebase

Before start coding, we will spend some time setting up our Firebase's push notifications service and real-time database to better understand what kind of data we will be dealing with in our app.

In summary, we will go through the following topics in this lesson:

- Complex Redux in React Native
- Firebase real-time database
- Firebase push notifications
- Firebase user management
- Forms

Let's start by reviewing the data models we will be using and how our app will connect with Firebase for syncing its data.

Firebase

Firebase is a **Mobile Backend as a Service (MBaaS)**, which means that it provides mobile developers with all the backend necessities, such as user management, no SQL database, and a push notification server. It integrates easily with React Native through an official node package, which brings the database connection for free. Unfortunately, Firebase doesn't offer a JavaScript SDK for their push notifications service, but there are several React Native libraries filling that gap by bridging Firebase's iOS and Java SDKs with a JavaScript interface. We will be using `react-native-fcm` as it is the most mature in its field.

Before building an app on top of a Firebase MBaaS, you need to create a project for it. This is a free process that is explained in Firebase's website `https://firebase.google.com/`. Although this process is not directly related to React Native, it's a good starting point to understand how to set up and use a MBaaS for our apps. Most of the configuring can be finished in a matter of minutes just by following the tutorials available on Firebase's documentation site. The benefits of setting up this MBaaS make those minutes worth the time and initial hassle.

To set up Firebase and connect our app to the correct project, we need to use the `configuration for the web` snippet we can find in the **Settings** screen inside our Firebase project's dashboard. We added this initialization snippet on `src/firebase.js`:

```
import firebase from 'firebase';

var firebaseConfig = {
  apiKey: "<Your Firebase API key>",
  authDomain: "<Your Firebase Auth domain>",
  databaseURL: "<Your Firebase database URL>",
  projectId: "<Your Firebase projectId>",
  storageBucket: "<Your Firebase storageBucket>",
  messagingSenderId: "<Your messaging SenderId>"
};

export const firebaseApp = firebase.initializeApp(firebaseConfig);
```

Once the project is set up, we can start taking a look at how our database is going to be structured.

Real-Time Database

Firebase allows mobile developers to store and sync data between users and devices in real time using a cloud-hosted, NoSQL database. Updated data syncs across connected devices in milliseconds and data remains available if your app goes offline, providing a great user experience regardless of network connectivity.

Three data models come into the picture when thinking about the basic data a one-to-one communication app should handle:

- `users`: This will store avatars, names, and push notification tokens. There is no need to store authentication data here as it is handled through a different Firebase API (authentication API).
- `messages`: We will save each message on each chat room separately for easy retrieval using the chat room ID as a key.
- `chats`: All the information about the opened chats will be stored here.

To understand how we will request and use the data in our app, let's see a gist of the example data we can actually use for testing:

```
{
  "chats" : {
    "--userId1--" : {
```

```
        "--userId2----userId1--" : {
          "contactId" : "--userId2--",
          "image" : "https://images.com/person2.jpg",
          "name" : "Jason"
        }
      },
      "--userId2--" : {
        "--userId2----userId1--" : {
          "contactId" : "--userId1--",
          "image" : "https://images.com/person1.jpg",
          "name" : "John"
        }
      }
    },
    "messages" : {
      "--userId2----userId1--" : {
        "-KpEwU8sr01vHSy3qvRY" : {
          "_id" : "2367ad00-301d-46b5-a7b5-97cb88781489",
          "createdAt" : 1500284842672,
          "text" : "Hey man!",
          "user" : {
            "_id" : "--userId2--",
            "name" : "Jason"
          }
        }
      }
    },
    "users" : {
      "--userId1--" : {
        "name" : "John",
        "notificationsToken" : ""
      },
      "--userId2--" : {
        "name" : "Jason",
        "notificationsToken" : "--notificationsId1--"
      }
    }
  }
}
```

We organized our data in a way it will be easy for the messaging app to retrieve and synchronize. Instead of normalizing the data structure, we introduced some data duplication to increase speed during data retrieval and simplify the frontend code to the maximum.

The `users` collection holds the users' data using the user ID as a key (`--user1--`, and `--user2--`). These user IDs are retrieved automatically by Firebase during registration/login. Each user has a notification token, which is an identifier for the device the user is logged in with the push notifications service. When the user logs out, the notifications token is removed, so messages sent to this user will be stored, but not notified to any device.

The `chats` collection stores each user's chat list by user ID. Each chat has its own ID (a concatenation of both user IDs) and will be duplicated as every user on that chat should have a copy of the chat data. In each copy, there is enough information for the other user to build up their chat screen.

The `messages` collection is stored in a separate collection, which can be referenced by that ID. Each chat ID points to a list of messages (only one in this example) where all the data needed by the chat screen is stored. There is also some duplication in this collection as some user data is stored together with each message to reduce the number of requests needed when building a chat screen.

A full tutorial on how to read and write data in Firebase's real-time database can be found on their website (`https://firebase.google.com/docs/database/`), but we will take a quick look at the methods we will be using in this lesson.

Reading Data from Firebase's Database

There are two ways for retrieving data from Firebase's database. The first one sets a listener that will be called every time the data changes, so we only need to set it up once for the entire lifetime of our app:

```
firebaseApp.database().ref('/users/' + userId).on('value', (snapshot)
=> {
  const userObj = snapshot.val();
  this.name = userObj.name;
  this.avatar = userObj.avatar;
});
```

As we can see, in order to retrieve a snapshot of data, we need to call the `database()` method in our `firebaseApp` object (the one we created in our `src/firebase.js` file). Then, we will have a `database` object where we can call the `ref('<uri>')` on it passing the URI, where the data is stored. That will return a reference to the piece of data pointed by that URI. We can go for the `on('value', callback)` method, which will attach a callback passing the snapshot of data. Firebase always returns objects as snapshots, so we need to transform them into plain data ourselves. In this example, we want to retrieve an object with two keys (`name` and `avatar`), so we only need to call the `val()` method on the snapshot to retrieve a plain object containing the data.

If we don't need the retrieved data to be automatically synched every time it is updated, we could have used the `once()` method instead of `on()`:

```
import firebase from 'firebase';
import { firebaseApp } from '../firebase';

firebaseApp.database().ref('/users/' + userId).once('value')
.then((snapshot) => {
  const userObj = snapshot.val();
  this.name = userObj.name;
  this.avatar = userObj.avatar;
});
```

The callback receiving snapshot will only be called once.

Updating Data in Firebase's Database

Writing data in a Firebase database can also be done in two different ways:

```
firebaseApp.database().ref('/users/' + userId).update({
  name: userName
});
```

The `update()` method changes the object referenced by the supplied URI according to the keys and values passed as a parameter. The rest of the object is left intact.

On the other hand, `set()` will replace the object in the database with the one we provide as a parameter:

```
firebaseApp.database().ref('/users/' + userId).set({
  name: userName,
  avatar: avatarURL
});
```

Finally, if we want to add a new snapshot of data but we want Firebase to generate an ID for it, we can use the `push` method:

```
firebaseApp.database().ref('/messages/' + chatId).push().set(message);
```

Authentication

We will use Firebase authentication services, so we don't need to worry about storing login credentials, handling forgotten passwords, or verifying emails on our side. These and other related tasks come for free with Firebase authentication services.

In order to activate login and registration through email and password, we need to enable this method as a session sign-in method in our Firebase dashboard. More information about how to do this can be found on Firebase's website at `https://firebase.google.com/docs/auth/web/password-auth`.

In our app, we only need to use the provided Firebase SDK for login:

```
firebase.auth().signInWithEmailAndPassword(username, password)
  .then(() => {
      //user is logged in
  })
  .catch(() => {
      //error logging in
  })
})
```

For registration, we can use the following code:

```
firebase.auth().createUserWithEmailAndPassword(email, password)
.then((user) => {
   //user is registered
})
.catch((error) => {
   //error registering
})
```

All the token handling will be taken care of by Firebase, and we only need to add a listener to make sure our app is updated when the authentication status changes:

```
firebase.auth().onAuthStateChanged((user) => {
  //user has logged in or out
}
```

Setting up the Folder Structure

Let's initialize a React Native project using React Native's CLI. The project will be named `messagingApp` and will be available for iOS and Android devices:

```
react-native init --version="0.45.1" messagingApp
```

We will be using MobX to manage state in our app, so we will need a folder for our stores. The rest of the folder structure is standard to most React apps.

We need five screens (Chats, Chat, Login, Profile, and Search), a component (ListItem) and two stores (chats and users), which will be available through the stores/index.js file. There are also two helpers that we will be using to support our app:

- notifications.js: All the logic related to push notifications will be stored in this file
- firebase.js: This includes the configuration and initialization of Firebase SDK

Since we will be using MobX and several other dependencies, let's take a look at our package.json file to understand what packages we will be using:

```
/*** package.json ***/

{
        "name": "messagingApp",
        "version": "0.0.1",
        "private": true,
        "scripts": {
                "start": "node node_modules/react-native/local-cli
                        /cli.js start",
                "test": "jest"
        },
        "dependencies": {
                "firebase": "^4.1.3",
                "mobx": "^3.2.0",
                "mobx-react": "^4.2.2",
                "react": "16.0.0-alpha.12",
                "react-native": "0.45.1",
                "react-native-fcm": "^7.1.0",
                "react-native-gifted-chat": "^0.2.0",
                "react-native-keyboard-aware-scroll-view": "^0.2.9",
                "react-native-vector-icons": "^4.2.0",
                "react-navigation": "^1.0.0-beta.11"
        },
        "devDependencies": {
                "babel-jest": "20.0.3",
                "babel-plugin-transform-decorators-legacy": "^1.3.4",
                "babel-preset-react-native": "2.1.0",
                "jest": "20.0.4",
                "react-test-renderer": "16.0.0-alpha.12"
        },
        "jest": {
```

```
                    "preset": "react-native"
          }
}
```

Some of the npm packages we will be using are:

- firebase: Firebase's SDK for authentication and database connection
- mobx: MobX will handle our app state
- react-native-fcm: Firebase's SDK for push messaging
- react-native-gifted-chat: A library for rendering chat rooms including date separation, avatars, and many other features
- react-native-keyboard-aware-scroll-view: A library that ensures the on-screen keyboard doesn't hide any focused text input when working with forms
- react-native-vector-icons: We will use Font Awesome icons for this app
- react-navigation: We will have a drawer, a tabbed, and a stack navigator handling the screens in our app
- babel-plugin-transform-decorators-legacy: This library allows us to use decorators (with the legacy @ syntax) which is quite useful when working with MobX

After running npm install, we will have our app ready to start coding. As it happened in previous apps, the entry point for our messaging app will be the same code both in index.ios.js for iOS and in index.android.js for Android:

```
/*** index.ios.js and index.android.js ***/

import React from 'react'
import { AppRegistry } from 'react-native';
import App from './src/main';

import { Provider } from 'mobx-react/native';
import { chats, users } from './src/stores';

class MessagingApp extends React.Component {
  render() {
    return (
      <Provider users={users} chats={chats}>
        <App/>
      </Provider>
    )
  }
```

```
}

AppRegistry.registerComponent('messagingApp', () => MessagingApp);
```

This is a standard way to start up a React Native app working with MobX--a
<Provider /> is supplied as the root element to inject the two stores (users and
chats) into the screens in our app. All the initializing and navigation logic has been
deferred to the src/main.js file:

```
/*** src/main.js ***/

import React from 'react'
import { DrawerNavigator,TabNavigator } from 'react-navigation'
import { Platform, View } from 'react-native'
import { observer, inject } from 'mobx-react/native'

import Login from './screens/Login'
import Chats from './screens/Chats'
import Profile from './screens/Profile'
import Search from './screens/Search'
import { users, chats } from './stores'

let Navigator;
if(Platform.OS === 'ios'){
  Navigator = TabNavigator({
    Chats: { screen: Chats },
    Search: { screen: Search },
    Profile: { screen: Profile }
  }, {
    tabBarOptions: {
      inactiveTintColor: '#aaa',
      activeTintColor: '#000',
      showLabel: true
    }
  });
} else {
  Navigator = DrawerNavigator({
    Chats: { screen: Chats },
    Search: { screen: Search },
    Profile: { screen: Profile }
  });
}

@inject('users') @observer
export default class App extends React.Component {
```

```
constructor() {
  super();
}

render() {
  if(this.props.users.isLoggedIn){
    return <Navigator/>
  } else {
    return <Login/>
  }
}
}
```

The first thing we can see on the `src/main.js` file is that we will use different navigators, depending on which platform we are running the app: iOS will open a tabbed navigator, while Android will open a drawer-based navigator.

Then, we see a line we will be repeating in many components in our app:

```
@inject('users') @observer
```

This is the way to tell MobX this component needs to receive the `users` store. MobX will then pass it as a prop to this component and therefore we can use all the methods and attributes it holds. In this case, we are interested in the `isLoggedIn` attribute to present the user with the `<Login />` screen if they are still not logged in. Since MobX will inject this attribute as a property in our component, the right way to access it will be `this.props.users.isLoggedIn`.

Before continuing building components, let's take a look at the stores we will be using throughout this lesson to better understand what data and actions are available.

Users Store

This store is responsible for holding all the data and logic surrounding users, but also helps the chats store initializing when a user is logged in:

```
/*** src/stores/users.js ***/

import {observable, computed, map, toJS, action} from 'mobx';
import chats from './chats'
import firebase from 'firebase';
import { firebaseApp } from '../firebase';
import notifications from '../notifications'
```

```
class Users {
        @observable id = null;
        @observable isLoggedIn = false;
        @observable name = null;
        @observable avatar = null;
        @observable notificationsToken = null;
        @observable loggingIn = false;
        @observable registering = false;
        @observable loggingError = null;
        @observable registeringError = null;

        @action login = function(username, password) {
                //login with Firebase email/password method
        }

        @action logout = function() {
                //logout from Firebase authentication service
        }

        @action register = function(email, password, name) {
                //register through firebase authentication service
        }

        @action setNotificationsToken(token) {
                //store the notifications token for this device
        }

        searchUsers(name) {
                //helper for searching users by name in the database
        }

        constructor() {
                this.bindToFirebase();
        }

        bindToFirebase() {
                //Initialise connection to Firebase user
                //authentication status and data
        }
}

const users = new Users();

export default users;
```

These are all the attributes and methods we need for this store. There are several flags (those attributes containing a verb in its -ing form) to note network activity. Let's implement each method now:

```
@action login = function(username, password) {
        this.loggingIn = true;
        this.loggingError = null;
        firebase.auth().signInWithEmailAndPassword(username, password)
        .then(() => {
                this.loggingIn = false;
                notifications.init((notificationsToken) => {
                        this.setNotificationsToken(notificationsTok
en);
                });
        })
        .catch((error) => {
                this.loggingIn = false;
                this.loggingError = error.message;
        });
}
```

Logging in with Firebase is as simple as calling `signInWithEmailAndPassword` on their authentication SDK. If the login is successful, we will initialize the notifications module to enable the device to receive push notifications. We will follow the opposite path on logout:

```
@action logout = function() {
        notifications.unbind();
        this.setNotificationsToken('');
        firebase.auth().signOut();
}
```

In the registration action, besides setting the appropriate flags for network activity, we need to validate the user entered a name, initialize the notifications, and store the name in the database:

```
@action register = function(email, password, name) {
        if(!name || name == '') {
                this.registering = false;
                this.registeringError = 'Name was not entered';
                return;
        }
        this.registering = true;
        this.registeringError = null;
        firebase.auth().createUserWithEmailAndPassword(email,
password)
```

```
        .then((user) => {
                this.registering = false;
                notifications.init((notificationsToken) => {
                        this.setNotificationsToken(notificationsTok
en);
                });
                firebaseApp.database().ref('/users/' + user.uid).set({
                        name: name
                });
        })
        .catch((error) => {
                this.registering = false;
                this.registeringError = error.message;
        })
}
```

Setting the notification token is just a simple update in the database:

```
@action setNotificationsToken(token) {
        if(!this.id) return;
        this.notificationsToken = token;
        firebaseApp.database().ref('/users/' + this.id).update({
                notificationsToken: token
        });
}
```

The searchUsers() method is not marked as @action, as it won't modify the state of our app, but only search and return a list of users with the provided name in the database:

```
searchUsers(name) {
        return new Promise(function(resolve) {
                firebaseApp.database().ref('/users/').once('value')
                .then(function(snapshot) {
                        let foundUsers = [];
                        const users = snapshot.val();
                        for(var id in users) {
                                if(users[id].name === name) {
                                        foundUsers.push({
                                                name: users[id].name,
                                                avatar:
                                                users[id].avatar,
                                                notificationsToken:
                                                users[id].
                                                notificationsToken,
                                                id
```

```
                                                });
                                        }
                                }
                                resolve(foundUsers);
                        });
                });
        }
```

We will return the result as a promise, due to the asynchronous nature of the request we are making.

Finally, `bindToFirebase()` will attach the attributes in this store to data snapshots in Firebase's database. This method is called by the constructor, so it serves as initialization for the user data. It's important to note that this data will be updated when the authentication status changed to always reflect the most up to date data for the user:

```
bindToFirebase() {
  return firebase.auth().onAuthStateChanged((user) => {
    if(this.chatsBind && typeof this.chatsBind.off === 'function')
      this.chatsBind.off();
    if(this.userBind && typeof this.userBind.off === 'function')
      this.userBind.off();

    if (user) {
      this.id = user.uid;
      this.isLoggedIn = true;
      this.chatsBind = chats.bindToFirebase(user.uid);
      this.userBind = firebaseApp.database().ref('/users/' + this.id).
                                        on('value', (snapshot) =>
      {
        const userObj = snapshot.val();
        if(!userObj) return;
        this.name = userObj.name;
        this.avatar = userObj.avatar;
      });
    } else {
      this.id = null;
      this.isLoggedIn = false;
      this.userBind = null;
      this.name = null;
      this.avatar = null;
    }
  });
}
```

We will store the listeners for the chat data (as `this.chatsBind`) and for the user data (as `this.userBind`), so we can remove them (by calling the `off()` method) before attaching new listeners on every `auth` state change.

Chats Store

This store is responsible for holding all the data and logic surrounding chats and messages, but it also helps the `chats` store initializing when a user is logged in:

```
/*** src/stores/chats.js ***/

import { observable, computed, map, toJS, action } from 'mobx';
import { AsyncStorage } from 'react-native'

import { firebaseApp } from '../firebase'
import notifications from '../notifications'

class Chats {
  @observable list;
  @observable selectedChatMessages;
  @observable downloadingChats = false;
  @observable downloadingChat = false;

  @action addMessages = function(chatId, contactId, messages) {
    //add a list of messages to a chat
  }

  @action selectChat = function(id) {
    //set a chat as selected and retrieve all the messages for it
  }

  @action add(user1, user2) {
    //add a new chat to the list of chats for the users in it
  }

  bindToFirebase(userId) {
    //listen for the list of chats in Firebase to update the
    @observable list
  }
}


const chats = new Chats()
export default chats;
```

We will store the list of open chats the user has in `@observable list`. When a user selects one chat, we will download and synchronize the list of messages on that chat to `@observable selectedChatMessages`. Then, we will have a couple of flags to let the user know when we are downloading data from the Firebase database.

Let's take a look at each method individually. We will start with `addMessages`:

```
@action addMessages = function(chatId, contactId, messages) {
  if(!messages || messages.length < 1) return;

  messages.forEach((message) => {
    let formattedMessage = {
      _id: message._id,
      user: {
        _id: message.user._id,
      }
    };
    if(message.text) formattedMessage.text = message.text;
    if(message.createdAt) formattedMessage.createdAt =
      message.createdAt/1;
    if(message.user.name) formattedMessage.user.name =
      message.user.name;
    if(message.user.avatar) formattedMessage.user.avatar =
      message.user.avatar;
    if(message.image) formattedMessage.image = message.image;

    //add the message to the chat
    firebaseApp.database().ref('/messages/' +
      chatId).push().set(formattedMessage);

    //notify person on the chat room
    firebaseApp.database().ref('/users/' + contactId).once('value')
    .then(function(snapshot) {
      var notificationsToken = snapshot.val().notificationsToken;
      notifications.sendNotification(notificationsToken, {
        sender: message.user.name,
        text: message.text,
        image: message.user.image,
        chatId
      });
    });
  });
}
```

This method receives three parameters:

- `chatId`: The ID for the chat in which the messages will be added.
- `contactId`: The ID for the user to whom we are sending the message. This will be used to send a notification to the user's contact.
- `messages`: This is an array with all the messages we want to add to the chat.

We will loop through the list of messages, formatting the message the way we want to store it. Then, we will call the `set()` method on a database reference to save the new message in Firebase's database. Finally, we need to send the notification to our contact, so we retrieve their notifications token by querying the `users` collection by their `contactId`.

Sending notifications is normally handled by the backend, but since we are setting all the logic on the app itself, we need to build a function to send notifications. We have done this in our notifications `module`: `notifications.sendNotification(notifi cationsToken, data);`.

Let's see what happens when we select a chat to display the messages for it:

```
@action selectChat = function(id) {
  this.downloadingChat = true;
  if(this.chatBind && typeof this.chatBind.off === 'function')
  this.chatBind.off();
  this.chatBind = firebaseApp.database().ref('/messages/' + id)
  .on('value', (snapshot) => {
    this.selectedChatMessages = [];
    this.downloadingChat = false;
    const messagesObj = snapshot.val();
    for(var id in messagesObj) {
      this.selectedChatMessages.push({
        _id: id,
        text: messagesObj[id].text,
        createdAt: messagesObj[id].createdAt,
        user: {
          _id: messagesObj[id].user._id,
          name: messagesObj[id].user.name,
          avatar: messagesObj[id].user.avatar
        },
        image: messagesObj[id].image
      });
    }
  });
}
```

The main piece of functionality here is attaching a listener to the messages/chat ID collection, which will sync the `this.selectedChatMessages` observable with the list of messages for the selected chat in the database. This means that every time a new message is stored in Firebase, `this.selectedChatMessages` will be synced to reflect it. This is how the `on()` method in the Firebase SDK works: we pass a callback, which we can use to synchronize the real-time database with our app's state.

Adding a new chat will be done using the `add()` method:

```
@action add(user1, user2) {
  return new Promise(function(resolve, reject) {
    firebaseApp.database().ref('/chats/' + user1.id + '/' + user1.id +
    user2.id).set({
      name: user2.name,
      image: user2.avatar,
      contactId: user2.id
    }).then(() => {
      firebaseApp.database().ref('/chats/' + user2.id + '/'
                                 + user1.id +
      user2.id).set({
        name: user1.name,
        image: user1.avatar,
        contactId: user1.id
      }).then(() => {
        resolve();
      })
    })
  });
}
```

Here, we are building and returning a promise that will be resolved when the two chats (one per each user participating in the chat) are updated. These two database updates can be seen as the duplication of data, but it will also reduce the data structure complexity and therefore our code base readability.

The last method in this store is `bindToFirebase()`:

```
bindToFirebase(userId) {
  this.downloadingChats = true;
  return firebaseApp.database().ref('/chats/' + userId).
                                on('value', (snapshot) => {
    this.downloadingChats = false;
    const chatsObj = snapshot.val();
    this.list = [];
    for(var id in chatsObj) {
```

```
      this.list.push({
        id,
        name: chatsObj[id].name,
        image: chatsObj[id].image,
        contactId: chatsObj[id].contactId
      });
    }
  });
}
```

As we saw in our `users` store, this method will be called when the user logs in and attaches a listener to the `chats/<userId>` snapshot of data to keep all the chats data synched with the database on the `this.list` attribute.

As a convenience, we will group both stores in `src/stores/index.js`, so we can import them both on one line of code:

```
/*** src/stores/index.js ***/

import users from './users';
import chats from './chats';

export {
  users,
  chats
};
```

This is all about the stores we will be using. As we can see, most of the business logic is handled here so it can be thoroughly tested. Let's move now to the helper we will use for notifications.

Push Notifications Using Firebase

Firebase incorporates a push notification service for iOS and Android, but it unfortunately doesn't provide any JavaScript on their SDK to use it. For this matter, an open source library was created bridging the Objective-C and Java SDKs into a React Native module: `react-native-fcm`.

We won't cover the installation of this module in this book, as it's a changing process that can be better followed on its repository at `https://github.com/evollu/react-native-fcm`.

We decided to abstract the logic for this module on our `src/notifications.js` file to make it available for every component while keeping its maintainability. Let's take a look at this file:

```
/*** src/notifications.js ***/

import {Platform} from 'react-native';
import FCM, {FCMEvent, RemoteNotificationResult,
WillPresentNotificationResult, NotificationType} from 'react-native-
fcm';

let notificationListener = null;
let refreshTokenListener = null;
const API_URL = 'https://fcm.googleapis.com/fcm/send';
const FirebaseServerKey = '<Your Firebase Server Key>';

const init = (cb) => {
  FCM.requestPermissions();
  FCM.getFCMToken().then(token => {
    cb(token)
  });
  refreshTokenListener = FCM.on(FCMEvent.RefreshToken, (token) => {
    cb(token);
  });
}

const onNotification = (cb) => {
  notificationListener = FCM.on(FCMEvent.Notification, (notif) => {
      cb(notif);

      if(Platform.OS ==='ios'){
        switch(notif._notificationType){
          case NotificationType.Remote:
            notif.finish(RemoteNotificationResult.NewData)
            break;
          case NotificationType.NotificationResponse:
            notif.finish();
            break;
          case NotificationType.WillPresent:
            notif.finish(WillPresentNotificationResult.All)
            break;
        }
      }
    })
  }
```

```
const unbind = () => {
  if(notificationListener) notificationListener.remove();
  if(refreshTokenListener) refreshTokenListener.remove();
}

const sendNotification = (token, data) => {
  let body = JSON.stringify({
    "to": token,
    "notification": {
                "title": data.sender || '',
                "body": data. text || '',
                "sound": "default"
        },
    "data": {
      "name": data.sender,
      "chatId": data.chatId,
      "image": data.image
    },
        "priority": 10
  });

  let headers = new Headers({
                "Content-Type": "application/json",
                "Content-Length": parseInt(body.length),
                "Authorization": "key=" + FirebaseServerKey
  });

  fetch(API_URL, { method: "POST", headers, body })
        .then(response => console.log("Send response", response))
        .catch(error => console.log("Error sending ", error));
}

export default { init, onNotification, sendNotification, unbind }
```

There are four functions exposed in this module:

- `init`: This requests the permission to receive push notifications (in case it was not yet granted) and requests the device token or refreshes it if changed.

- `onNotification`: This invokes a provided callback when a notification is received. In iOS, it also calls the appropriate methods on the notification to close the cycle.

- unbind: This stops listening for push notifications.
- sendNotification: This formats and sends a push notification to a specific device using a provided notifications token.

Sending notifications in Firebase can be done using their HTTP API, so we will use fetch for sending a POST request with the proper header and body data.

Now, we have all the logic we need to start building our screens and components.

Login

The <Login /> component heavily relies on the users store for logic, as it is mostly focused on rendering two forms for login and registration. All the validation for the forms is done by Firebase, so we only need to focus on rendering the UI elements and calling the proper store methods.

In this screen, we will be using the react-native-keyboard-aware-scroll view, which is a module providing a self-scrolling <Scrollview />, which reacts to any focused <TextInput /> so they are not hidden when the keyboard pops up.

Let's take a look at the code:

```
/*** src/screens/Login.js ***/


import React, { PropTypes } from 'react'
import {
  ScrollView,
  TextInput,
  Button,
  Text,
  View,
  Image,
  ActivityIndicator
} from 'react-native';
import { observer, inject } from 'mobx-react/native'
import Icon from 'react-native-vector-icons/FontAwesome'
import { KeyboardAwareScrollView } from 'react-native-keyboard-aware-
scroll-view'

import LoginForm from '../components/LoginForm'
import RegistrationForm from '../components/RegistrationForm'

@inject('users') @observer
```

```
class Login extends React.Component {
  onLogin(email, password) {
    this.props.users.login(email, password);
  }

  onPressRegister(email, password, name) {
    this.props.users.register(email, password, name);
  }

  render() {
    return (
      <KeyboardAwareScrollView style={{padding: 20, marginTop: 20,
        backgroundColor: '#eee'}}>
        <Icon name="comments" size={60} color='#ccc'
          style={{alignSelf: 'center', paddingBottom: 20}}/>
        <View style={{alignItems: 'center', marginBottom: 20}}>
          <Text>- please, login to continue -</Text>
        </View>
        <LoginForm
          onPress={this.onLogin.bind(this)}
          busy={this.props.users.loggingIn}
          loggingError={this.props.users.loggingError}
        />
        <View style={{alignItems: 'center', marginTop: 20,
                   marginBottom: 20}}>
          <Text>- or register -</Text>
        </View>
        <RegistrationForm
          onPress={this.onPressRegister.bind(this)}
          busy={this.props.users.registering}
          registeringError={this.props.users.registeringError}
        />
      </KeyboardAwareScrollView>
    )
  }
}

export default Login;
```

We split the login screen in two forms: `<LoginForm />` and `<RegistrationForm />`. Both components need to be passed three props:

- `onPress`: What the component needs to do when the **Send** button is pressed.

- busy: Are we waiting for remote data?
- loginError/registrationError: Description of the error that happened when logging/register (in case it happened).

We are wrapping the whole screen in a `<KeyboardAwareScrollView />` to ensure no `<TextInput />` gets hidden by the keyboard when focused. Let's take a look at the `LoginForm` now:

```
/*** src/components/LoginForm.js ***/

import React, { PropTypes } from 'react'
import {
  TextInput,
  Button,
  Text,
  View,
  Image,
  ActivityIndicator
} from 'react-native';

class LoginForm extends React.Component {
  state= {
    loginEmail: '',
    loginPassword: ''
  }

  onPressLogin() {
    this.props.onPress(this.state.loginEmail,
    this.state.loginPassword);
  }

  render() {
    return (
        <View style={{backgroundColor: 'white', padding: 15,
                    borderRadius: 10}}>
          {
            this.props.loggingError &&
            <View style={{backgroundColor: '#fcc', borderRadius: 5,
              alignItems: 'center', marginBottom: 10}}>
              <Text>{this.props.loggingError}</Text>
            </View>
          }
          <TextInput
            autoCapitalize='none'
```

```
          autoCorrect={false}
          keyboardType='email-address'returnKeyType='next'
          style={{height: 40}}
          onChangeText={(loginEmail) => this.setState({loginEmail})}
          value={this.state.loginEmail}
          placeholder='email'
          onSubmitEditing={(event) => {
            this.refs.loginPassword.focus();
          }}
        />
        <TextInput
          ref='loginPassword'
          style={{height: 40}}
          onChangeText={(loginPassword) =>
          this.setState({loginPassword})}
          value={this.state.loginPassword}
          secureTextEntry={true}
          placeholder='password'
        />
        {
          this.props.busy ?
          <ActivityIndicator/>
          :
          <Button
            onPress={this.onPressLogin.bind(this)}
            title='Login'
          />
        }
      </View>
    )
  }
}


export default LoginForm;
```

For the `<TextInput />` elements containing the email, we set the property `keyboardType='email-address'` so the @ sign is easily accessible on the software keyboard. There are other options such as numeric keyboards, but we will only use `'email-address'` for this app.

Another useful prop on `<TextInput />` is `returnKeyType`. We set `returnKeyType='next'` for those form inputs that are not the last ones to display the `Next` button in the keyboard so the user knows they can go to the next input by tapping that button. This prop is used in conjunction with a prop like the following:

```
onSubmitEditing={(event) => {
  this.refs.loginPassword.focus();
}}
```

`onSubmitEditing` is a `<TextInput />` prop that will be invoked when a user presses the `Return` or `Next` button on the keyboard. We are using it to focus on the next `<TextInput />`, which is quite user-friendly when dealing with forms. To get the reference for the next `<TextInput />` we use `ref`, which is not the safest way, but is good enough for simple forms. For this to work, we need to assign the corresponding `ref` to the next `<TextInput />`: `ref='loginPassword'`.

`RegistrationForm` is a very similar form:

```
/*** src/components/RegistrationForm ***/

import React, { PropTypes } from 'react'
import {
  ScrollView,
  TextInput,
  Button,
  Text,
  View,
  Image,
  ActivityIndicator
} from 'react-native';

class RegisterForm extends React.Component {
  state= {
    registerEmail: '',
    registerPassword: '',
    registerName: ''
  }

  onPressRegister() {
    this.props.onPress(this.state.registerEmail,
    this.state.registerPassword, this.state.registerName);
  }

  render() {
    return (
```

```
<View style={{backgroundColor: 'white', padding: 15,
          borderRadius: 10}}>
  {
    this.props.registeringError &&
    <View style={{backgroundColor: '#fcc', borderRadius: 5,
      alignItems: 'center', marginBottom: 10}}>
      <Text>{this.props.registeringError}</Text>
    </View>
  }
  <TextInput
    autoCapitalize='none'
    autoCorrect={false}
    keyboardType='email-address'
    returnKeyType='next'
    style={{height: 40}}
    onChangeText={(registerEmail) =>
    this.setState({registerEmail})}
    value={this.state.registerEmail}
    placeholder='email'
    onSubmitEditing={(event) => {
      this.refs.registerName.focus();
    }}
  />
  <TextInput
    ref='registerName'
    style={{height: 40}}
    onChangeText={(registerName) =>
    this.setState({registerName})}
    returnKeyType='next'
    value={this.state.registerName}
    placeholder='name'
    onSubmitEditing={(event) => {
      this.refs.registerPassword.focus();
    }}
  />
  <TextInput
    ref='registerPassword'
    style={{height: 40}}
    onChangeText={(registerPassword) =>
    this.setState({registerPassword})}
    value={this.state.registerPassword}
    secureTextEntry={true}
    placeholder='password'
  />
```

```
        {
          this.props.busy ?
          <ActivityIndicator/>
          :
          <Button
            onPress={this.onPressRegister.bind(this)}
            title='Register'
          />
        }
      </View>
    )
  }
}

export default RegisterForm;
```

Chats

This is the screen displaying the list of open chats. The special thing to note here is we are using a second navigator to display selected chats on top of the chats list. This means we need a `StackNavigator` in our `Chats` component that will contain two screens: `ChatList` and `Chat`. When a user taps on a chat from `ChatList`, `StackNavigator` will display the selected chat on top of `ChatList` making the list of chats available through a standard `< back` button in the header.

For listing the chats, we will use `<FlatList />`, a performant interface for rendering simple, flat lists, supporting the most of the features from `<ListView />`:

```
/*** src/screens/Chats.js ***/

import React, { PropTypes } from 'react'
import { View, Text, FlatList, ActivityIndicator } from 'react-native'
import { observer, inject } from 'mobx-react/native'
import { StackNavigator } from 'react-navigation'
import Icon from 'react-native-vector-icons/FontAwesome'
import notifications from '../notifications'

import ListItem from '../components/ListItem'
import Chat from './Chat'

@inject('chats') @observer
class ChatList extends React.Component {
  imgPlaceholder =
  'https://cdn.pixabay.com/photo/2017/03/21/02/00/user-
```

```
                      2160923_960_720.png'

componentWillMount() {
  notifications.onNotification((notif)=>{
    this.props.navigation.goBack();
    this.props.navigation.navigate('Chat', {
      id: notif.chatId,
      name: notif.name || '',
      image: notif.image || this.imgPlaceholder
    })
  });
}


render () {
  return (
    <View>
      {
        this.props.chats.list &&
        <FlatList
          data={this.props.chats.list.toJS()}
          keyExtractor={(item, index) => item.id}
          renderItem={({item}) => {
            return (
              <ListItem
                text={item.name}
                image={item.image || this.imgPlaceholder}
                onPress={() => this.props.navigation.
navigate('Chat',
                {
                  id: item.id,
                  name: item.name,
                  image: item.image || this.imgPlaceholder,
                  contactId: item.contactId
                })}
              />
            )
          }}
        />
      }
      {
        this.props.chats.downloadingChats &&
        <ActivityIndicator style={{marginTop: 20}}/>
      }
    </View>
```

```
      )
    }
  }

  const Navigator = StackNavigator({
    Chats: {
      screen: ChatList,
      navigationOptions: ({navigation}) => ({
        title: 'Chats',
      }),
    },
    Chat: {
      screen: Chat
    }
  });

  export default class Chats extends React.Component {
    static navigationOptions = {
      tabBarLabel: 'Chats',
      tabBarIcon: ({ tintColor }) => (
        <Icon name="comment-o" size={30} color={tintColor}/>
      )
    };

    render() {
        return <Navigator />
    }
  }
```

The first thing we notice is that we are injecting the `chats` store where the list of chats is saved: `@inject('chats')` `@observer`. We need this to build our `<FlatList />`, based on `this.props.chats.list`, but as the list of chats is an observable MobX object, we need to transform it using its `toJS()` method to make a JavaScript array out of it.

On the `componentWillMount()` function, we will invoke `onNotification` on the notifications module to open the corresponding chat every time the user presses a push notification on her device. Therefore, we will use the `navigate()` method on the navigator to open the proper chat screen including the name of the contact and her avatar.

ListItem

The list of chats relies on `<ListItem />` to render each specific chat within the list. This component is a custom UI class we created to reduce the `ChatList` component complexity:

```
/*** src/components/ListItem.js ***/

import React, { PropTypes } from 'react'
import { View, Image, Text, TouchableOpacity } from 'react-native'
import Icon from 'react-native-vector-icons/FontAwesome'

const ListItem = (props) => {
  return (
    <TouchableOpacity onPress={props.onPress}>
      <View style={{height: 60, borderColor: '#ccc',
                borderBottomWidth: 1,
        marginLeft: 10, flexDirection: 'row'}}>
        <View style={{padding: 15, paddingTop: 10}}>
          <Image source={{uri: props.image}} style={{width: 40,
                                                height: 40,
            borderRadius: 20, resizeMode: 'cover'}}/>
        </View>
        <View style={{padding: 15, paddingTop: 20}}>
          <Text style={{fontSize: 15}}>{ props.text }</Text>
        </View>
        <Icon name="angle-right" size={20} color="#aaa"
          style={{position: 'absolute', right: 20, top: 20}}/>
      </View>
    </TouchableOpacity>
  )
}

export default ListItem
```

There is little logic on this component as it only receives a prop named `onPress()`, which will be called when the `<ListItem />` is pressed, which, as we saw on this component's parent, will open the chat screen to show the list of messages on that specific chat. Let's take a look at the `chat` screen where all the messages for a specific chat are rendered.

Chat

To keep our code succinct and maintainable, we will use GiftedChat for rendering all the messages in a chat, but there is still some work we need to do to properly render this screen:

```
/*** src/screens/Chat.js ***/

import React, { PropTypes } from 'react'
import { View, Image, ActivityIndicator } from 'react-native';
import { observer, inject } from 'mobx-react/native'
import { GiftedChat } from 'react-native-gifted-chat'

@inject('chats', 'users') @observer
class Chat extends React.Component {
  static navigationOptions = ({ navigation, screenProps }) => ({
    title: navigation.state.params.name,
    headerRight: <Image source={{uri: navigation.state.params.image}}
    style={{
      width: 30,
      height: 30,
      borderRadius: 15,
      marginRight: 10,
      resizeMode: 'cover'
    }}/>
  })

  onSend(messages) {
    this.props.chats.addMessages(this.chatId, this.contactId,
    messages);
  }

  componentWillMount() {
    this.contactId = this.props.navigation.state.params.contactId;
    this.chatId = this.props.navigation.state.params.id;this.props.
chats.selectChat(this.chatId);
  }

  render () {
    var messages = this.props.chats.selectedChatMessages;
    if(this.props.chats.downloadingChat) {
      return <View><ActivityIndicator style={{marginTop: 20}}/></View>
    }
```

```
      return (
        <GiftedChat
          onSend={(messages) => this.onSend(messages)}
          messages={messages ? messages.toJS().reverse() : []}
          user={{
            _id: this.props.users.id,
            name: this.props.users.name,
            avatar: this.props.users.avatar
          }}
        />
      )
    }
  }
```

```
  export default Chat;
```

We also need to inject some stores for our `<Chat />` component to work. This time, we need `users` and `chats` stores that will be available as props inside the component. This component also expects to receive two params from the navigator: `chatId` (the ID for the chat) and `contactId` (the ID for the person the user is chatting with).

When the component is getting ready to be mounted (`onComponentWillMount()`) we save the `chatId` and `contactId` in more convenient variables inside the component and call the `selectChat()` method on the `chats` store. This will trigger a request to Firebase database to fetch the messages for the selected chat, which will be synced through the `chats` store and is accessible to the component through `this.props.chats.selectedChatMessages`. MobX will also update a `downloadingChat` property to ensure we let the user know the data is being retrieved from Firebase.

Lastly, we need to add a `onSend()` function to `GiftedChat`, which will call the `addMessages()` method on the `chats` store to post the message to Firebase every time the `Send` button is pressed.

`GiftedChat` helped us in largely reducing the amount of work we need to do in order to render the list of messages for a chat. On the other hand, we had to format the messages in the way `GiftedChat` requires and provide an `onSend()` function to be executed whenever we need a message posted to our backend.

Search

The search screen is divided into two parts: a `<TextInput />` for the user to search a name and a `<FlatList />` to show the list of contacts found with the entered name:

```
import React, { PropTypes } from 'react'
import { View, TextInput, Button, FlatList } from 'react-native'
import Icon from 'react-native-vector-icons/FontAwesome'
import { observer, inject } from 'mobx-react/native'

import ListItem from '../components/ListItem'

@inject('users', 'chats') @observer
class Search extends React.Component {
  imgPlaceholder = 'https://cdn.pixabay.com/photo/2017/03/21/02/00/
user-
                   2160923_960_720.png'

  state = {
    name: '',
    foundUsers: null
  }

  static navigationOptions = {
    tabBarLabel: 'Search',
    tabBarIcon: ({ tintColor }) => (
      <Icon name="search" size={30} color={tintColor}/>
    )
  };

  onPressSearch() {
    this.props.users.searchUsers(this.state.name)
    .then((foundUsers) => {
      this.setState({ foundUsers });
    });
  }

  onPressUser(user) {
    //open a chat with the selected user
  }

  render () {
    return (
      <View>
        <View style={{padding: 20, marginTop: 20,
```

```
                    backgroundColor: '#eee'}}>
        <View style={{backgroundColor: 'white', padding: 15,
                    borderRadius: 10}}>
          <TextInput
            style={{borderColor: 'gray', borderBottomWidth: 1,
                    height: 40}}
            onChangeText={(name) => this.setState({name})}
            value={this.state.name}
            placeholder='Name of user'
          />
          <Button
            onPress={this.onPressSearch.bind(this)}
            title='Search'
          />
        </View>
      </View>
      {
        this.state.foundUsers &&
        <FlatList
          data={this.state.foundUsers}
          keyExtractor={(item, index) => index}
          renderItem={({item}) => {
            return (
              <ListItem
                text={item.name}
                image={item.avatar || this.imgPlaceholder}
                onPress={this.onPressUser.bind(this, item)}
              />
            )
          }}
        />
      }
    </View>
    )
  }
}

export default Search;
```

This component requires the injection of both stores (users and chats). The users store is used to invoke the searchUsers() method when the user hits the Search button. This method doesn't modify the state and therefore we need to provide a callback to receive the list of found users to finally set that list on the component's state.

The second store, `chats`, will be used to store the open chat in Firebase by calling `add()` from the `onPressUser()` function:

```
onPressUser(user) {
  this.props.chats.add({
    id: this.props.users.id,
    name: this.props.users.name,
    avatar: this.props.users.avatar || this.imgPlaceholder,
    notificationsToken: this.props.users.notificationsToken || ''
  }, {
    id: user.id,
    name: user.name,
    avatar: user.avatar || this.imgPlaceholder,
    notificationsToken: user.notificationsToken || ''
  });

  this.props.navigation.navigate('Chats', {});
}
```

The `add()` method in the `chats` store requires two parameters to be passed: one per each user in the newly open chat. This data will be properly stored in Firebase, so both users will see the chat on their chat list in the app. After adding the new chat, we will navigate the app to the chats screen so the user can see if the addition was successful.

Profile

The profile screen displays the user's avatar, name, and a `Logout` button for signing out:

```
import React, { PropTypes } from 'react'
import { View, Image, Button, Text } from 'react-native'
import { observer, inject } from 'mobx-react/native'
import Icon from 'react-native-vector-icons/FontAwesome'

import notifications from '../notifications'

@inject('users') @observer
class Profile extends React.Component {
  static navigationOptions = {
    tabBarLabel: 'Profile',
    tabBarIcon: ({ tintColor }) => (
      <Icon name="user" size={30} color={tintColor}/>
    ),
```

```
    };

    imgPlaceholder =
    'https://cdn.pixabay.com/photo/2017/03/21/02/00/user-
                    2160923_960_720.png'

    onPressLogout() {
      this.props.users.logout();
    }

    render () {
      return (
          <View style={{ padding: 20 }}>
            {
                this.props.users.name &&
                <View style={{ flexDirection: 'row', alignItems:
    'center'
            }}>
                  <Image
                    source={{uri: this.props.users.avatar ||
                    this.imgPlaceholder}}
                    style={{width: 100, height: 100, borderRadius: 50,
                        margin: 20, resizeMode: 'cover'}}
                  />
                  <Text style={{fontSize: 25}}>{this.props.users.name}
                  </Text>
                </View>
            }
            <Button
              onPress={this.onPressLogout.bind(this)}
              title="Logout"
            />
          </View>
      )
    }
  }

  export default Profile;
```

The logout process is triggered by calling the `logout()` method on the `users` store. Since we controlled the authentication status in our `src/main.js` file, the app will automatically return to the **Login** or **Register** screen when the logout is successful.

Summary

We covered several important topics for most of the modern enterprise apps: user management, data synchronization, complex app state, and handling forms. This is a complete app, which we manage to fix with a small code base and the help of MobX and Firebase.

Firebase is very capable of handling this app in production with a large number of users, but building our own backend system should not be a complex task, especially if we have experience in working with socket.io and real-time databases.

There are some aspects missing in this lesson such as handling security (which can be done fully within Firebase) or creating chat rooms for more than two users. In any case, these aspects fall out of React Native's environment, so they were intentionally left out.

After finishing this lesson, we should be able to build any app on top of Firebase and MobX as we covered the most used user cases on both pieces of technology. Of book, there are some more complex cases that were left out, but they can be easily learned by having a good understanding of the basics explained throughout this lesson.

In the next lesson, we will build a very different kind of app: a game written in React Native.

Assessments

1. This ____ store is responsible for holding all the data and logic surrounding chats and messages, and also helps the chats store initializing when a user is logged in.

    1. Push notification
    2. List
    3. Chats
    4. Search

2. Which of the following is the main function to calculate the new position for each sprite stored in the sprites.

    1. `getRockProps()`
    2. `reducer()`
    3. `action()`
    4. `moveSprites()`

3. State whether the following statement is True or False: Firebase allows mobile developers to store and sync data between users and devices in real time using a cloud-hosted, NoSQL database.

4. The background image is not contained in any custom component but in _____. This is because it doesn't need any special logic being a static element.

    1. `<GamseContainer />`

    2. `<Image />`

    3. `<TouchableWithoutFeedback />`

    4. `<TouchableOpacity />`

5. What are the available Redux actions?

4
Project 4 – Game

Most of the most successful apps on the app stores are games. They proved to be really popular as mobile users tend to play all sort of games while commuting, in waiting rooms, when traveling, or even when relaxing at home. It is a fact that mobile users are more inclined to pay for a game than for any other kind of app in the market as the perceived value is higher most of the time.

Modern games are usually built in powerful gaming engines such as Unity or Unreal, as they provide a wide range of tools and frameworks to work with sprites, animations, or physics. But the reality is that great games can also be built in React Native due to its native capabilities. Moreover, React Native has introduced many web and mobile app programmers into game development as it offers them a familiar and intuitive interface. Of book, there are some concepts in game development which need to be understood in order to make the most of the library when building games. Concepts like sprites, ticks, or collisions are small hurdles, which may need to be overcome by non-game developers before building a game.

The game will be built for both iOS and Android, and will use a limited number of external libraries. Redux, the state management library, was chosen to help calculate the position of every sprite on each frame.

We will use some custom sprites and add a sound effect to notice each time the score is increased. One of the main challenges when building a game is making sure the sprites are rendered responsively, so different devices will show the game with the same proportions providing the same game experience across different screen sizes.

This game will be designed to be played in portrait mode only.

Overview

The game we will build in this lesson has simple mechanics:

- The goal is to help a parrot fly between rocks in a cave
- Tapping the screen will result in the parrot flying higher
- Gravity will pull the parrot toward the ground
- Any collision between the parrot and the rocks or the ground will result in the end of the game
- The score will be increased every time the parrot flies through a group of rocks

This kind of game is very well suited to being built with React Native, as it doesn't really need complex animations or physics capabilities. All we need to be sure of is that we move every sprite (graphics component) on the screen at the correct time to create the feeling of continuous animation.

Let's take a look at the initial screen for our game:

This screen presents the logo and instructions about how to get the game started. In this case, a simple tap will start up the game mechanics causing the parrot to fly forward and up on every tap.

The player must help our parrot to fly through the rocks. Each time a set of rocks is passed, the player will get one point.

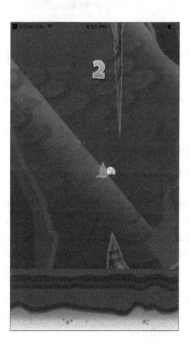

To make it more difficult, the heights of the rocks will vary forcing the parrot to fly higher or lower to pass through the rocks. If the parrot collides with a rock or the ground, the game will stop and the final score will be presented to the user:

At this point, the user will be able to restart the game by tapping again on the screen.

To make it nicer and easier to play, tapping can be done anywhere on the screen, causing a different effect depending on which screen the user is on:

- On the initial screen tapping will start up the game
- In-game tapping will result in the parrot flying higher
- On the **GAME OVER** screen tapping will restart the game and reset the score

As can be observed, it will be a very simple game but, due to this, easily extendable and fun to play. One import aspect when building this kind of app is counting with a nice set of graphics. For this matter, we will download our assets from one of the multiple game assets markets, which can be found online (most game assets cost a small amount of money although free assets can be found every now and then).

The technical challenges for this game lie more in how the sprites will be moved over time than on a complex state to be maintained. Despite this, we will use Redux to keep and update the app's state as it is a performant and well-known solution. Besides revisiting Redux, we will review the following topics in this lesson:

- Handling animated sprites
- Playing sound effects
- Detecting colliding sprites
- Absolute positioning in different screen resolutions

Sprites

Sprites are the graphics used by the games, normally grouped into one or several images. Many game engines include tools to split and manage those graphics in a convenient way, but this is not the case in React Native. Since it was designed with a different kind of app having in mind, there are several libraries supporting React Native in the task of dealing with sprites, but our game will be simple enough not to need any of these libraries, so we will store one graphic in each image and we will load them separately into the app.

Before starting to build the game, let's get acquainted with the graphics we will load, as they will be the building blocks for the whole app.

Numbers

Instead of using a `<Text/>` component to display the score in our game, we will use sprites for a more attractive look. These are the images we will use to represent the user's score:

As mentioned, all these graphics will be stored in separate images (named `0.png` to `9.png`) due to React Native's lack of sprite splitting capabilities.

Background

We need a large background to make sure it will fit all screen sizes. In this lesson, we will use this sprite as a static graphic although it could be easily animated to create a nice parallax effect:

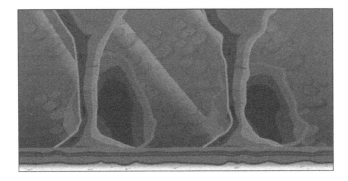

From this background, we will take a piece of ground to animate.

Ground

The ground will be animated in a loop to create a constant feeling of velocity. The size of this image needs to be larger than the maximum screen resolution we want to support, as it should be moved from one side of the screen to the opposite. At all times, two ground images will be displayed, one after the other to ensure at least one of them is shown on the screen during the animation:

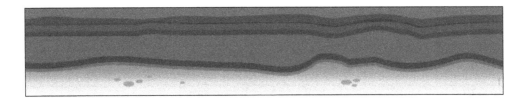

Rocks

The moving rocks are the obstacles our parrot needs to pass. There will be one on the top and one on the bottom and both will be animated at the same speed as the ground. Their height will vary for each pair of rocks but always keep the same gap size between them:

In our `images` folder, we will have `rock-up.png` and `rock-down.png` representing each sprite.

Parrot

We will use two different images for our main character so we can create an animation displaying when the user has tapped on the screen:

The first image will be displayed when the parrot is moving down:

This second image will be shown every time the user presses the screen to move the parrot up. The images will be named `parrot1.png` and `parrot2.png`.

The Home Screen

For the home screen, we will display two images: a logo and some instructions about how to get the game started. Let's take a look at them:

The instructions to start the game just point out that tapping will get the game started:

Game Over Screen

When the parrot hits a rock or the ground, the game will end. Then, it is time to display a game over sign and a reset button to get the game started again:

Although the entire screen will be touchable to get the game restarted, we will include a button to let the user know that tapping will result in the game restarting:

This image will be stored as `reset.png`.

This is the full list of images we will have in our game:

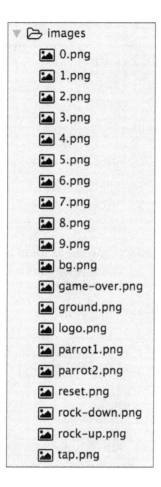

Now, we know the list of images we will use in our game. Let's take a look at the whole folder structure.

Setting up the folder structure

Let's initialize a React Native project using React Native's CLI. The project will be named `birdGame` and will be available for iOS and Android devices:

```
react-native init --version="0.46.4" birdGame
```

As this one is a simple game, we will only need one screen in which we will position all our sprites moving, showing, or hiding them depending on the state of the game, which will be managed by Redux. Therefore, our folder structure will be in line the standard Redux apps:

The `actions` folder will only contain one file as there are only three actions which may happen in this game (`start`, `tick`, and `bounce`). There is also a `sounds` folder to store the sound effect which will be played every time the parrot passes a pair of rocks:

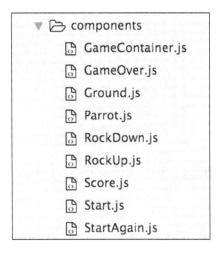

For each sprite, we will create a component so we can move it, show it, or hide it easily:

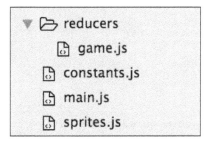

Again, only one reducer will be needed to process all our actions. We will also create two helper files:

- `constants.js`: This is where we will store helper variables for dividing the height and the width of the screen for the device playing the game
- `sprites.js`: This stores all the functions which will calculate how the sprites should be positioned in each frame to create the required animations

`main.js` will serve as the entry point for both iOS and Android and will be responsible to initialize Redux:

The rest of the files are generated by React Native's CLI.

Let's now review the `package.json` file we will need to set the dependencies up in our project:

```
/*** package.json ***/

{
  "name": "birdGame",
  "version": "0.0.1",
  "private": true,
  "scripts": {
    "start": "node node_modules/react-native/local-cli/cli.js start",
    "test": "jest"
  },
  "dependencies": {
    "react": "16.0.0-alpha.12",
    "react-native": "0.46.4",
    "react-native-sound": "^0.10.3",
    "react-redux": "^4.4.5",
    "redux": "^3.5.2"
  },
  "devDependencies": {
    "babel-jest": "20.0.3",
    "babel-preset-react-native": "2.1.0",
    "jest": "20.0.4",
    "react-test-renderer": "16.0.0-alpha.12"
  },
  "jest": {
    "preset": "react-native"
  }
}
```

Apart from Redux libraries, we will import `react-native-sound`, which will be in charge of playing any sounds in our game.

After running `npm install`, we will have our app ready to start coding. As happened in previous apps, the entry point for our messaging app will be the same code both in `index.ios.js` for iOS and in `index.android.js` for Android, but both will delegate the initialisation logic to `src/main.js`:

```
/*** index.ios.js and index.android.js ***/

import { AppRegistry } from 'react-native';
import App from './src/main';

AppRegistry.registerComponent('birdGame', () => App);
```

`src/main.js` is responsible for initializing Redux and will set `GameContainer` as the root component in our app:

```
/*** src/main.js ***/

import React from "react";
import { createStore, combineReducers } from "redux";
import { Provider } from "react-redux";

import gameReducer from "./reducers/game";
import GameContainer from "./components/GameContainer";

let store = createStore(combineReducers({ gameReducer }));

export default class App extends React.Component {
  render() {
    return (
      <Provider store={store}>
        <GameContainer />
      </Provider>
    );
  }
}
```

We use `GameContainer` as the root of the component tree in our app. As a regular Redux app, a `<Provider />`component is in charge of supplying the store to all the components which require reading or modifying the application state.

GameContainer

`GameContainer` is responsible for starting up the game once the user taps the screen. It will do this using `requestAnimationFrame()`--one of the custom timers implemented in React Native.

`requestAnimationFrame()` is similar to `setTimeout()`, but the former will fire after all the frame has flushed, whereas the latter will fire as quickly as possible (over 1000x per second on a iPhone 5S); therefore, `requestAnimationFrame()` is more suited for animated games as it deals only with frames.

As happens with most animated games, we need to create a loop to animate the sprites in the screen by calculating the next position of each element on each frame. This loop will be created by a function named `nextFrame()` inside our `GameContainer`:

```
nextFrame() {
```

```
if (this.props.gameOver) return;
    var elapsedTime = new Date() - this.time;
    this.time = new Date();
    this.props.tick(elapsedTime);
this.animationFrameId =
    requestAnimationFrame(this.nextFrame.bind(this));
}
```

This function will be aborted if the property `gameOver` is set to `true`. Otherwise, it will trigger the action `tick()` (which calculates how the sprites should be moved on to the next frame, based on the elapsed time) and finally calls itself through `requestAnimationFrame()`. This will keep the loop in the game to animate the moving sprites.

Of book, this `nextFrame()` should be called at the start for the first time, so we will also create a `start()` function inside `GameContainer` to get the game started:

```
start() {
cancelAnimationFrame(this.animationFrameId);
    this.props.start();
    this.props.bounce();
    this.time = new Date();
    this.setState({ gameOver: false });
this.animationFrameId =
    requestAnimationFrame(this.nextFrame.bind(this));
}
```

The `start` function makes sure there is no animation started by calling `cancelAnimationFrame()`. This will prevent any double animations being performed when the user resets the game.

Then, the functions trigger the `start()` action, which will just set a flag in the store to notice the game has started.

We want to start the game by moving the parrot up, so the user has the time to react. For this, we also call the `bounce()` action.

Finally, we start the animation loop by passing the already known `nextFrame()` function as a callback of `requestAnimationFrame()`.

Let's also review the `render()` method we will use for this container:

```
render() {
    const {
      rockUp,
      rockDown,
```

```
        ground,
        ground2,
        parrot,
        isStarted,
        gameOver,
        bounce,
        score
    } = this.props;

    return (
        <TouchableOpacity
onPress={
            !isStarted || gameOver ? this.start.bind(this) :
              bounce.bind(this)
        }
        style={styles.screen}
activeOpacity={1}
        >
        <Image
          source={require("../../images/bg.png")}
          style={[styles.screen, styles.image]}
        />
        <RockUp
          x={rockUp.position.x * W} //W is a responsiveness factor
                                    //explained in the 'constants'
section
          y={rockUp.position.y}
          height={rockUp.size.height}
          width={rockUp.size.width}
        />
        <Ground
          x={ground.position.x * W}
          y={ground.position.y}
          height={ground.size.height}
          width={ground.size.width}
        />
        <Ground
          x={ground2.position.x * W}
          y={ground2.position.y}
          height={ground2.size.height}
          width={ground2.size.width}
        />
        <RockDown
          x={rockDown.position.x * W}
```

```
            y={rockDown.position.y * H} //H is a responsiveness factor
                                       //explained in the 'constants'
                                       //section
        height={rockDown.size.height}
        width={rockDown.size.width}
      />
      <Parrot
        x={parrot.position.x * W}
        y={parrot.position.y * H}
        height={parrot.size.height}
        width={parrot.size.width}
      />
      <Score score={score} />
      {!isStarted && <Start />}
      {gameOver && <GameOver />}
      {gameOver && isStarted && <StartAgain />}
    </TouchableOpacity>
  );
}
```

It may be lengthy, but actually, it's a simple positioning of all the visible elements on the screen while wrapping them in a `<TouchableOpacity />` component to capture the user tapping no matter in which part of the screen. This `<TouchableOpacity />` component is actually not sending any feedback to the user when they tap the screen (we disabled it by passing `activeOpacity={1}` as a prop) since this feedback is already provided by the parrot bouncing on each tap.

 We could have used React Native's `<TouchableWithoutFeedback />` for this matter, but it has several limitations which would have harmed our performance.

The provided `onPress` attribute just defines what the app should do when the user taps on the screen:

- If the game is active, it will bounce the parrot sprite
- If the user is on the game over screen it will restart the game by calling the `start()` action

All other children in the `render()` method are the graphic elements in our game, specifying for each of them, their position and size. It's also important to note several points:

- There are two `<Ground />` components because we need to continuously animate it in the *x* axis. They will be positioned one after the other horizontally to animate them together so when the end of the first `<Ground />` component is shown on screen, the beginning of the second will follow creating the sense of continuum.

- The background is not contained in any custom component but in `<Image />`. This is because it doesn't need any special logic being a static element.

- Some positions are multiplied by factor variables (`W` and `H`). We will take a deeper look at these variables in the constants section. At this point, we only need to know that they are variables helping in the absolute positioning of the elements taking into account all screen sizes.

- Let's now put all these functions together to build up our `<GameContainer />`:

```
/*** src/components/GameContainer.js ***/

import React, { Component } from "react";
import { connect } from "react-redux";
import { bindActionCreators } from "redux";
import { TouchableOpacity, Image, StyleSheet } from "react-native";

import * as Actions from "../actions";
import { W, H } from "../constants";
import Parrot from "./Parrot";
import Ground from "./Ground";
import RockUp from "./RockUp";
import RockDown from "./RockDown";
import Score from "./Score";
import Start from "./Start";
import StartAgain from "./StartAgain";
import GameOver from "./GameOver";

class Game extends Component {
constructor() {
    super();
    this.animationFrameId = null;
    this.time = new Date();
  }
```

```
    nextFrame() {
      ...
    }

    start() {
      ...
    }

  componentWillUpdate(nextProps, nextState) {
      if (nextProps.gameOver) {
        this.setState({ gameOver: true });
        cancelAnimationFrame(this.animationFrameId);
      }
    }

  shouldComponentUpdate(nextProps, nextState) {
      return !nextState.gameOver;
    }

    render() {

      ...

    }
  }

  const styles = StyleSheet.create({
    screen: {
      flex: 1,
      alignSelf: "stretch",
      width: null
    },
    image: {
      resizeMode: "cover"
    }
  });

  function mapStateToProps(state) {
    const sprites = state.gameReducer.sprites;
    return {
parrot: sprites[0],
      rockUp: sprites[1],
      rockDown: sprites[2],
```

```
      gap: sprites[3],
      ground: sprites[4],
      ground2: sprites[5],
      score: state.gameReducer.score,
      gameOver: state.gameReducer.gameOver,
      isStarted: state.gameReducer.isStarted
    };
}
function mapStateActionsToProps(dispatch) {
    return bindActionCreators(Actions, dispatch);
}

export default connect(mapStateToProps, mapStateActionsToProps)
(Game);
```

We added three more ES6 and React lifecycle methods to this component:

- `super()`: The constructor will save an attribute named `animationFrameId` to capture the ID for the animation frame in which the `nextFrame` function will run and also another attribute named `time` will store the exact time at which the game was initialized. This `time` attribute will be used by the `tick()` function to calculate how much the sprites should be moved.

- `componentWillUpdate()`: This function will be called every time new props (positions and sizes for the sprites in the game) are passed. It will detect when the game must be stopped due to a collision so the game over screen will be displayed.

- `shouldComponentUpdate()`: This performs another check to avoid re-rendering the game container if the game has ended.

The rest of the functions are Redux related. They are in charge of connecting the component to the store by injecting actions and attributes:

- `mapStateToProps()`: This gets the data for all the sprites in the store and injects them into the component as props. The sprites will be stored in an array and therefore they will be accessed by index. On top of these, the `Score`, a flag noting if the current game is over, and a flag noting if the game is in progress will also be retrieved from the state and injected into the component.

- `mapStateActionsToProps()`: This will inject the three available actions (`tick`, `bounce`, and `start`) into the component so they can be used by it.

Accessing the sprites data by index is not a recommended practice as indexes can change if the number of sprites grows, but we will use it like this in this app for simplicity reasons.

Actions

As we mentioned before, only three Redux actions will be available:

- `tick()`: To calculate the next position of the sprites on the screen
- `bounce()`: To make the parrot fly up
- `start()`: To initialize the game variables

This means our `src/actions/index.js` file should be very simple:

```
/*** src/actions/index.js ***/

export function start() {
  return { type: "START" };
}

export function tick(elapsedTime) {
  return { type: "TICK", elapsedTime };
}

export function bounce() {
  return { type: "BOUNCE" };
}
```

Only the `tick()` action needs to pass a payload: the time it passed since the last frame.

Reducer

Since we have a very limited amount of actions, our reducer will also be fairly simple and will delegate most of the functionality to the sprites helper functions in the `src/sprites.js` file:

```
/*** src/reducers/index.js ***/

import {
  sprites,
  moveSprites,
```

```
    checkForCollision,
    getUpdatedScore,
    bounceParrot
} from "../sprites";

const initialState = {
  score: 0,
  gameOver: false,
  isStarted: false,
  sprites
};

export default (state = initialState, action) => {
  switch (action.type) {
    case "TICK":
      return {
        ...state,
        sprites: moveSprites(state.sprites, action.elapsedTime),
        gameOver: checkForCollision(state.sprites[0],
        state.sprites.slice(1)),
        score: getUpdatedScore(state.sprites, state.score)
      };
    case "BOUNCE":
      return {
        ...state,
        sprites: bounceParrot(state.sprites)
      };
    case "START":
      return {
        ...initialState,
        isStarted: true
      };
    default:
      return state;
  }
};
```

The start() function only needs to set the isStarted flag to true, as the initial state will have it set to false by default. We will reuse this initial state every time the game ends.

bounce() will use the bounceParrot() function from the sprites module to set a new direction for the main character.

The most important changes will happen when the `tick()` function is triggered, as it needs to calculate the positions of all moving elements (through the `moveSprites()` function), detect if the parrot has collided with any static elements (through the `checkForCollision()` function), and update the score in the store (through the `getUpdatedScore()` function).

As we can see, most of the game's functionality is delegated to the helper functions inside the sprites module, so let's take a deeper look into the `src/sprites.js` file.

The Sprites Module

The structure of the sprites module is formed by an array of sprites and several exported functions:

```
/*** src/sprites.js ***/

import sound from "react-native-sound";

const coinSound = new sound("coin.wav", sound.MAIN_BUNDLE);
let heightOfRockUp = 25;
let heightOfRockDown = 25;
let heightOfGap = 30;
let heightOfGround = 20;

export const sprites = [
    ...
];

function prepareNewRockSizes() {
    ...
}

function getRockProps(type) {
    ...
}

export function moveSprites(sprites, elapsedTime = 1000 / 60) {
    ...
}

export function bounceParrot(sprites) {
    ...
}
```

```
function hasCollided(mainSprite, sprite) {
  ...
}

export function checkForCollision(mainSprite, sprites) {
  ...
}

export function getUpdatedScore(sprites, score) {
  ...
}
```

This module begins by loading the sound effect we will play when the parrot passes a set of rocks to give feedback to the user about the increment in their score.

Then, we define some heights for several sprites:

* `heightOfRockUp`: This is the height of the rock which will appear in the upper part of the screen.

* `heightOfRockDown`: This is the height of the rock which will show in the lower part of the screen.

* `heightOfGap`: We will create an invisible view between the upper and the lower rock to detect when the parrot has passed each set of rocks so the score is updated. This this gap's height.

* `heightOfGround`: This is a static value for the height of the ground.

Each other item in this module plays a role in moving or positioning the sprites on the screen.

The Sprites Array

This is the array in charge of storing all the sprite's positions and sizes at a given time. Why are we using an array for storing our sprites instead of a hash map (Object)? Mainly for extensibility; although a hash map would make our code noticeably more readable, if we want to add new sprites of an existing type (as it happens with the `ground` sprite in this app) we would need to use artificial keys for each of them despite being the same type. Using an array of sprites is a recurrent pattern in game development which allows to decouple the implementation from the list of sprites.

Whenever we want to move a sprite, we will update its position in this array:

```
export const sprites = [
  {
```

```
      type: "parrot",
      position: { x: 50, y: 55 },
      velocity: { x: 0, y: 0 },
      size: { width: 10, height: 8 }
    },
    {
      type: "rockUp",
      position: { x: 110, y: 0 },
      velocity: { x: -1, y: 0 },
      size: { width: 15, height: heightOfRockUp }
    },
    {
      type: "rockDown",
      position: { x: 110, y: heightOfRockUp + 30 },
      velocity: { x: -1, y: 0 },
      size: { width: 15, height: heightOfRockDown }
    },
    {
      type: "gap",
      position: { x: 110, y: heightOfRockUp },
      velocity: { x: -1, y: 0 },
      size: { width: 15, height: 30 }
    },
    {
      type: "ground",
      position: { x: 0, y: 80 },
      velocity: { x: -1, y: 0 },
      size: { width: 100, height: heightOfGround }
    },
    {
      type: "ground",
      position: { x: 100, y: 80 },
      velocity: { x: -1, y: 0 },
      size: { width: 100, height: heightOfGround }
    }
  ];
```

The array will store the initial values for positioning and sizing all the moving sprites in the game.

prepareNewRockSizes()

This function randomly calculates the size of the next upper and lower rock together with the height of the gap between them:

```
function prepareNewRockSizes() {
  heightOfRockUp = 10 + Math.floor(Math.random() * 40);
  heightOfRockDown = 50 - heightOfRockUp;
  heightOfGap = 30;
}
```

It's important to note that this function only calculates the heights for the new set of rocks but doesn't create them. This is just a preparation step.

getRockProps()

The helper functions to format the position and size attributes of a rock (or gap):

```
function getRockProps(type) {
  switch (type) {
    case "rockUp":
      return { y: 0, height: heightOfRockUp };
    case "rockDown":
      return { y: heightOfRockUp + heightOfGap,
               height: heightOfRockDown };
    case "gap":
      return { y: heightOfRockUp, height: heightOfGap };
  }
}
```

moveSprites()

This is the main function as it calculates the new position for each sprite stored in the sprites array. Game development relies in physics to calculate the position for each sprite in each frame.

For example, if we want to move an object to the right side of the screen, we will need to update its x position a number of pixels. The more pixels we add to the object's x attribute for the next frame, the faster it will move (sprite.x = sprite.x + 5; moves sprite five times faster than sprite.x = sprite.x + 1;).

As we can see in the following example, the way we calculate the new position for each sprite is based on three factors: the current position of the sprite, the time that has passed since the last frame (elapsedTime), and the gravity/velocity of the sprite (i.e. sprite.velocity.y + elapsedTime * gravity).

Additionally, we will use the helper function `getRockProps` to get the new sizes and positions for the rocks. Let's take a look at how the `moveSprites` function looks like:

```
export function moveSprites(sprites, elapsedTime = 1000 / 60) {
  const gravity = 0.0001;
  let newSprites = [];

  sprites.forEach(sprite => {
    if (sprite.type === "parrot") {
      var newParrot = {
        ...sprite,
        position: {
          x: sprite.position.x,
          y:
            sprite.position.y +
            sprite.velocity.y * elapsedTime +
            0.5 * gravity * elapsedTime * elapsedTime
        },
        velocity: {
          x: sprite.velocity.x,
          y: sprite.velocity.y + elapsedTime * gravity
        }
      };
      newSprites.push(newParrot);
    } else if (
      sprite.type === "rockUp" ||
      sprite.type === "rockDown" ||
      sprite.type === "gap"
    ) {
      let rockPosition,
        rockSize = sprite.size;
      if (sprite.position.x > 0 - sprite.size.width) {
        rockPosition = {
          x: sprite.position.x + sprite.velocity.x,
          y: sprite.position.y
        };
      } else {
        rockPosition = { x: 100, y: getRockProps(sprite.type).y };
        rockSize = { width: 15,
                     height: getRockProps(sprite.type).height };
      }
      var newRock = {
        ...sprite,
        position: rockPosition,
```

```
          size: rockSize
        };
        newSprites.push(newRock);
      } else if (sprite.type === "ground") {
        let groundPosition;
        if (sprite.position.x > -97) {
          groundPosition = { x: sprite.position.x + sprite.velocity.x,
                             y: 80 };
        } else {
          groundPosition = { x: 100, y: 80 };
        }
        var newGround = { ...sprite, position: groundPosition };
        newSprites.push(newGround);
      }
    });
    return newSprites;
}
```

Calculating the next position for a sprite is, most of the time, basic addition (or subtraction). Let's take, for example, how the parrot should move:

```
var newParrot = {
        ...sprite,
        position: {
          x: sprite.position.x,
          y:
            sprite.position.y +
            sprite.velocity.y * elapsedTime +
            0.5 * gravity * elapsedTime * elapsedTime
        },
        velocity: {
          x: sprite.velocity.x,
          y: sprite.velocity.y + elapsedTime * gravity
        }
      }
```

The parrot will only move vertically, basing its speed on gravity, so the x attribute will always stay fixed for it while the y attribute will change according to the function `sprite.position.y` + `sprite.velocity.y` * `elapsedTime` + 0.5 * `gravity` * `elapsedTime` * `elapsedTime` which, in summary, adds the elapsed time and the gravity in different factors.

The calculations for how the rocks should move are a little more complex, as we need to take into account every time the rocks disappear from the screen (`if (sprite.position.x > 0 - sprite.size.width)`). As they have been passed, we need to recreate them with different heights (`rockPosition = { x: 100, y: getRockProps(sprite.type).y }`).

We have the same behavior for the ground, in terms of having to recreate it once it abandons the screen completely (`if (sprite.position.x > -97)`).

bounceParrot()

The only task for this function is changing the velocity of the main character, so it will fly up reversing the effect of gravity. This function will be called whenever the user taps on the screen while the game is started:

```
export function bounceParrot(sprites) {
  var newSprites = [];
  var sprite = sprites[0];
  var newParrot = { ...sprite, velocity: { x: sprite.velocity.x,
                    y: -0.05 } };
  newSprites.push(newParrot);
  return newSprites.concat(sprites.slice(1));
}
```

It's a simple operation in which we take the parrot's sprite data from the `sprites` array; we change its velocity on the **y** axis to a negative value so that the parrot moves upwards.

checkForCollision()

`checkForCollision()` is responsible for identifying if any of the rigid sprites have collided with the parrot sprite, so the game can be stopped. It will use `hasCollided()` as a supporting function to perform the required calculations on each specific sprite:

```
function hasCollided(mainSprite, sprite) {
  /***
   *** we will check if 'mainSprite' has entered in the
   *** space occupied by 'sprite' by comparing their
   *** position, width and height
   ***/

  var mainX = mainSprite.position.x;
  var mainY = mainSprite.position.y;
```

```
var mainWidth = mainSprite.size.width;
var mainHeight = mainSprite.size.height;

var spriteX = sprite.position.x;
var spriteY = sprite.position.y;
var spriteWidth = sprite.size.width;
var spriteHeight = sprite.size.height;

/***
 *** this if statement checks if any border of mainSprite
 *** sits within the area covered by sprite
 ***/

if (
  mainX < spriteX + spriteWidth &&
  mainX + mainWidth > spriteX &&
  mainY < spriteY + spriteHeight &&
  mainHeight + mainY > spriteY
) {
  return true;
}
}

export function checkForCollision(mainSprite, sprites) {
  /***
   *** loop through all sprites in the sprites array
   *** checking, for each of them, if there is a
   *** collision with the mainSprite (parrot)
   ***/

  return sprites.filter(sprite => sprite.type !== "gap").find(sprite
=> {
    return hasCollided(mainSprite, sprite);
  });
}
```

For simplicity, we assume that all sprites have a rectangular shape (even though rocks grow thinner towards the end) because the calculation would be a lot more complex if we considered different shapes.

In summary, `checkForCollision()` is just looping through the `sprites` array to find any colliding sprite, `hasCollided()` checks for collisions based on the sprite size and position. In just an `if` statement, we compare the boundaries of a sprite and the parrot's sprite to see if any of those boundaries are occupying the same area of the screen.

getUpdatedScore()

The last function in the sprites module will check if the score needs to be updated based on parrot position relative to the gap position (the gap between the upper and the lower rock is also counted as a sprite):

```
export function getUpdatedScore(sprites, score) {
  var parrot = sprites[0];
  var gap = sprites[3];

  var parrotXPostion = parrot.position.x;
  var gapXPosition = gap.position.x;
  var gapWidth = gap.size.width;

  if (parrotXPostion === gapXPosition + gapWidth) {
    coinSound.play();
    score++;
    prepareNewRockSizes();
  }

  return score;
}
```

An `if` statement checks if the parrot's position in the **x** axis has surpassed the gap (`gapXPosition + gapWidth`). When this happens, we play the sound we created in the header of the module (`const coinSound = new sound("coin.wav", sound.MAIN_BUNDLE);`) by calling its `play()` method. Moreover, we will increase the `score` variable and prepare a new set of rocks to be rendered when the current ones leave the screen.

Constants

We already saw the variables `W` and `H`. They represent one part of the screen if we divided it into 100 parts. Let's take a look at the `constants.js` file to understand this better:

```
/*** src/constants.js ***/

import { Dimensions } from "react-native";

var { width, height } = Dimensions.get("window");

export const W = width / 100;
export const H = height / 100;
```

W can be calculated as the total width of the device's screen divided by 100 units (as percentages are easier to reason about when positioning our sprites). The same goes for H; it can be calculated by dividing the total height by 100. Using these two constants, we can position and size our sprites relative to the size of the screen, so all screen sizes will display the same ratios for positions and sizes.

These constants will be used in all the visual components requiring responsive capabilities so they will show and move different depending on the screen size. This technique will ensure the game is playable even in small screens as the sprites will be resized accordingly.

Let's move on now to the components which will be displayed inside the `<GameContainer />`.

Parrot

The main character will be represented by this component, which will comprise of two different images (the same parrot with its wings up and down) driven by the Y position property passed by `<GameContainer />`:

```
/*** src/components/parrot.js ***/

import React from "react";
import { Image } from "react-native";
import { W, H } from "../constants";

export default class Parrot extends React.Component {
  constructor() {
    super();
    this.state = { wings: "down" };
  }

  componentWillUpdate(nextProps, nextState) {
    if (this.props.y < nextProps.y) {
      this.setState({ wings: "up" });
    } else if (this.props.y > nextProps.y) {
      this.setState({ wings: "down" });
    }
  }

  render() {
    let parrotImage;
    if (this.state.wings === "up") {
      parrotImage = require("../../images/parrot1.png");
```

```
      } else {
        parrotImage = require("../../images/parrot2.png");
      }
      return (
        <Image
          source={parrotImage}
          style={{
            position: "absolute",
            resizeMode: "contain",
            left: this.props.x,
            top: this.props.y,
            width: 12 * W,
            height: 12 * W
          }}
        />
      );
    }
  }
```

We use a state variable named `wings` to pick which image the parrot will be--when it is flying up the image with the wings down will be displayed while the wings up will be shown when flying down. The way this will be calculated is based on the position of the bird on the **y** axis passed as a property from the container:

- If the `Y` position is lower than the previous `Y` position means the bird is going down and therefore the wings should be up
- If the `Y` position is higher than the previous `Y` position means the bird is going up and therefore the wings should be down

The size of the parrot is fixed to `12 * W` both for the `height` and `width` as the sprite is a square and we want it to be sized relative to the width of each screen device.

RockUp and RockDown

The sprites for the rocks have no logic on them and are basically `<Image />` components positioned and sized by the parent component. This is the code for `<RockUp />`:

```
/*** src/components/RockUp.js ***/

import React, { Component } from "react";
import { Image } from "react-native";

import { W, H } from "../constants";
```

```
export default class RockUp extends Component {
  render() {
    return (
      <Image
        resizeMode="stretch"
        source={require("../../images/rock-down.png")}
        style={{
          position: "absolute",
          left: this.props.x,
          top: this.props.y,
          width: this.props.width * W,
          height: this.props.height * H
        }}
      />
    );
  }
}
```

The height and the width will be calculated by the following formulae: `this.props.width * W` and `this.props.height * H`. This will size the rock relative to the device's screen and the provided height and width.

The code for `<RockDown />` is quite similar:

```
/*** src/components/RockDown.js ***/

import React, { Component } from "react";
import { Image } from "react-native";

import { W, H } from "../constants";

export default class RockDown extends Component {
  render() {
    return (
      <Image
        resizeMode="stretch"
        source={require("../../images/rock-up.png")}
        style={{
          position: "absolute",
          left: this.props.x,
          top: this.props.y,
          width: this.props.width * W,
          height: this.props.height * H
        }}
```

```
        />
      );
    }
  }
```

Ground

Building the ground component is similar to the rock sprites. An image rendered in the proper position and size will be sufficient for this component:

```
/*** src/components/Ground.js ***/

import React, { Component } from "react";
import { Image } from "react-native";

import { W, H } from "../constants";

export default class Ground extends Component {
  render() {
    return (
      <Image
        resizeMode="stretch"
        source={require("../../images/ground.png")}
        style={{
          position: "absolute",
          left: this.props.x,
          top: this.props.y * H,
          width: this.props.width * W,
          height: this.props.height * H
        }}
      />
    );
  }
}
```

In this case, we will use H to relatively positioning the ground image.

Score

We decided to use number images to render the score, so we will need to load them and pick the appropriate digits depending on the user's score:

```
/*** src/components/Score.js ***/

import React, { Component } from "react";
import { View, Image } from "react-native";

import { W, H } from "../constants";

export default class Score extends Component {
getSource(num) {
    switch (num) {
      case "0":
        return require("../../images/0.png");
      case "1":
        return require("../../images/1.png");
      case "2":
        return require("../../images/2.png");
      case "3":
        return require("../../images/3.png");
      case "4":
        return require("../../images/4.png");
      case "5":
        return require("../../images/5.png");
      case "6":
        return require("../../images/6.png");
      case "7":
        return require("../../images/7.png");
      case "8":
        return require("../../images/8.png");
      case "9":
        return require("../../images/9.png");
      default:
        return require("../../images/0.png");
    }
  }

  render() {
    var scoreString = this.props.score.toString();
    var scoreArray = [];
    for (var index = 0; index < scoreString.length; index++) {
```

```
        scoreArray.push(scoreString[index]);
    }

    return (
      <View
        style={{
          position: "absolute",
          left: 47 * W,
          top: 10 * H,
          flexDirection: "row"
        }}
      >
        {scoreArray.map(
          function(item, i) {
            return (
              <Image
                style={{ width: 10 * W }}
                key={i}
                resizeMode="contain"
                source={this.getSource(item)}
              />
            );
          }.bind(this)
        )}
      </View>
    );
  }
}
```

We are doing the following in the `render` method:

- Converting the score to a string
- Converting the string into a list of digits
- Turning this list of digits into a list of images using the supporting `getSource()` function

One of the limitations in React Native `<Image />` is that its source cannot be required as a variable. Hence, we are using this small trick of retrieving the source from our `getSource()` method, which actually acquires all the possible images and returns the correct one through a `switch`/`case` clause.

Start

The start screen includes two images:

- A logo

- A start button explaining how to start up the game (tapping anywhere on the screen)

```
/*** src/components/Start.js ***/

import React, { Component } from "react";
import { Text, View, StyleSheet, Image } from "react-native";

import { W, H } from "../constants";

export default class Start extends Component {
  render() {
    return (
      <View style={{ position: "absolute", left: 20 * W, top: 3 *
H }}>
        <Image
          resizeMode="contain"
          source={require("../../images/logo.png")}
          style={{ width: 60 * W }}
        />
        <Image
          resizeMode="contain"
          style={{ marginTop: 15, width: 60 * W }}
          source={require("../../images/tap.png")}
        />
      </View>
    );
  }
}
```

We are using our H and W constants again to ensure the elements are positioned in the right place on every device screen.

GameOver

When the parrot collides with a rock or the ground, we should display the game over screen. This screen only contains two images:

- A game over sign
- A button to restart the game

Let's first take a look at the game over sign:

```
/*** src/components/GameOver.js ***/

import React, { Component } from "react";
import { Image } from "react-native";

import { W, H } from "../constants";

export default class GameOver extends Component {
  render() {
    return (
      <Image
        style={{
          position: "absolute",
          left: 15 * W,
          top: 30 * H
        }}
        resizeMode="stretch"
        source={require("../../images/game-over.png")}
      />
    );
  }
}
```

Now, let's move on to the reset the game button.

StartAgain

Actually, the reset button is only a sign as the user will be able to tap not only on the button but anywhere on the screen to get the game started. In any case, we will position this button properly on every screen using the *H* and *W* constants:

```
/*** src/components/StartAgain.js ***/

import React, { Component } from "react";
```

```
import { Text, View, StyleSheet, TouchableOpacity, Image }
from "react-native";

import { W, H } from "../constants";

export default class StartAgain extends Component {
  render() {
    return (
      <Image
        style={{ position: "absolute", left: 35 * W, top: 40 * H }}
        resizeMode="contain"
        source={require("../../images/reset.png")}
      />
    );
  }
}
```

Summary

Games are a very special kind of app. They are based on displaying and moving sprites on the screen, depending on the time and the user interaction. That is why we spent most of this lesson explaining how we could easily display all the images in the most performant way and how to position and size them.

We also reviewed a common trick to position and size sprites relatively to the height and width of the device screen.

Despite not being designed for games specifically, Redux was used to store and distribute the sprite's data around the components in our app.

At a general level, we proved that React Native can be used to build performant games and, although it lacks game-specific tooling, we can produce a very readable code which means it should be easy to extend and maintain. In fact, some very easy extensions can be created at this stage to make the game more fun and playable: increase speed after passing a specific amount of obstacles, reduce or increase the gap size, show more than one set of rocks on screen at once, and so.

With this, we've come to the end of this learning journey. I hope you'd a smooth journey and gained a lot of knowledge on React.

I wish you all the best for your future projects. Keep learning and exploring!

Assessments

1. Name the graphics that are used by the games, normally grouped into one or several images.

   1. Numbers

   2. Background

   3. Ground

   4. Sprites

2. State whether the following statement is True or False: Sprites are the graphics used by the games, normally grouped into one or several images. Many game engines include tools to split and manage those graphics in a convenient way, but this is not the case in React Native.

3. State whether the following statement is True or False: The sprites array is the array in charge of storing all the sprite's positions and sizes at a given time.

4. Which functions are in charge of connecting the component to the store by injecting actions and attributes?

5. _____ is responsible for starting up the game once the user taps the screen. It will do this using `requestAnimationFrame()`--one of the custom timers implemented in React Native.

   1. `nextFrame()`

   2. `cancelAnimationFrame()`

   3. `GameContainer`

   4. `mapStateToProps(state)`

Assessment Answers

Lesson 1: Project 1 – Car Booking App

Question Number	Answer
1	2
2	1
3	3
4	4
5	<ul><li>`shadowColor`: This adds the hexadecimal or RGBA value of the color we want for our component</li><li>`shadowOffset`: This shows how far we want our shadow to be casted</li><li>`shadowRadius`: This shows the value of the radius in the corner of our shadow</li><li>`shadowOpacity`: This shows how dark we want our shadow to be</li></ul>

Lesson 2: Project 2 – Image Sharing App

Question Number	Answer
1	2
2	1
3	True
4	3

5	• onPress: What the component needs to do when the **Send** button is pressed • busy: This means "Are we waiting for remote data?" • loginError/ registrationError: Description of the error that happened when logging/register (in case it happened)

Lesson 3: Project 3 – Messaging App

Question Number	Answer
1	3
2	4
3	True
4	2
5	• tick(): To calculate the next position of the sprites on the screen • bounce(): To make the parrot fly up • start(): To initialize the game variables

Lesson 4: Project 4 – Game

Question Number	Answer
1	4
2	True
3	True

4	<ul><li>`mapStateToProps()`: This gets the data for all the sprites in the store and injects them into the component as props. The sprites will be stored in an array and therefore they will be accessed by an index. On top of these, the Score, a flag noting if the current game is over and a flag noting if the game is in progress, will also be retrieved from the state and injected into the component.</li><li>`mapStateActionsToProps()`: This will inject the three available actions (`tick`, `bounce`, and `start`) into the component so they can be used by it.</li></ul>
5	3

www.ingramcontent.com/pod-product-compliance
Lightning Source LLC
Chambersburg PA
CBHW080530060326
40690CB00022B/5085